MUSIC IN EVERY CLASSROOM

MUSIC IN EVERY CLASSROOM
A Resource Guide for Integrating Music Across the Curriculum, Grades K-8

James Douglas Sporborg

1998
LIBRARIES UNLIMITED, INC.
and Its Division
Teacher Ideas Press
Englewood, Colorado

Copyright © 1998 Libraries Unlimited, Inc.
All Rights Reserved
Printed in the United States of America

No part of this publication may be reproduced, stored in a retrieval system, or transmitted, in any form or by any means, electronic, mechanical, photocopying, recording, or otherwise, without the prior written permission of the publisher.

LIBRARIES UNLIMITED, INC.
and Its Division
Teacher Ideas Press
P.O. Box 6633
Englewood, CO 80155-6633
1-800-237-6124
www.lu.com
www.lu.com/tip

Production Editor: Kay Mariea
Copy Editor: Shannon Graff
Proofreader: Cherie Rayburn
Layout and Design: Pamela J. Getchell

Library of Congress Cataloging-in-Publication Data

Sporborg, James Douglas.
  Music in every classroom : a resource guide for integrating music across the curriculum, grades K-8 / James Douglas Sporborg.
    xiii, 127 p. 17x25 cm.
    Includes indexes.
    ISBN 1-56308-610-7
    1. School music--Instruction and study--Bibliography.   I. Title.
ML128.S25S66 1998
016.37287'044--dc21   98-19823
                                                            CIP
                                                            MN

CONTENTS

Acknowledgments ix
Preface xi

♪ LANGUAGE ARTS 1
Language 1
Literature 2
Reading 2
Writing 3

♪ MATHEMATICS 5
General 6
Fractions 7

♪ SCIENCE 9
General 9
Animals 10
Environment 12
Physics 15
    Sound 15
Plants 16
Technology 17
    Instrument Building 17

♪ SOCIAL STUDIES 19
African Americans 19
American History 23
    General 23
    Colonial Period 28
    American Revolution 30
    The Federal Period (1786–1801) 34
    War of 1812 35

SOCIAL STUDIES (continued)

American History (continued)
    Industrial Revolution 36
    Westward Expansion 36
    The Gold Rush 40
    Immigration 41
    Slavery 42
    The Civil War and Reconstruction 44
    The Great Depression and World War II 48
    Post World War II 50
    Civil Rights Movement 51
    Vietnam War 53
Geography 53
    Land Forms 53
Government 54
    Constitution and Bill of Rights 54
    Elections 55
Holidays 55
Local History 56
Native Americans 57
Occupations 59
    General 59
    Cowboys 61
    Farmers 63
    Lumbermen 65
    Mill (Textile) Workers 66
    Miners 67
    Sailors 68
    Soldiers 70
    Whalers 71
Regions 72
    General 72
    The Great Lakes 73
    The Great Plains 73
    New England 75
    The South 76
    The Southwest 78
    The West 78
States 79
    Alabama 79
    California 80
    Connecticut 80
    Florida 80
    Idaho 80
    Illinois 80
    Indiana 81
    Kentucky 81

Louisiana	81
Maine	82
Maryland	82
Massachusetts	82
Michigan	82
Mississippi	83
Missouri	83
New Hampshire	83
New Mexico	83
New York	83
North Carolina	84
Ohio	85
Pennsylvania	85
South Carolina	85
Tennessee	85
Utah	86
Vermont	86
Virginia	87
West Virginia	87
Wisconsin	87
Transportation	88
General	88
Canalboats	88
Railroad	89
Riverboats	91
Ships	92
Women's History	93
World Cultures	94
General	94
Africa	99
Asia	100
Canada	102
Europe	103
India	105
Latin America and the Caribbean	106
Puerto Rico	108
Middle East	109
Author/Title Index	111
Subject Index	123

ACKNOWLEDGMENTS

This work was begun in a research course in partial fulfillment of the requirements for the degree of Master of Library Science at Southern Connecticut State University. I would especially like to thank Victor Triolo for his support and suggestions. I would also like to thank other members of the Department of Library Science and Instructional Technology, Arlene Bielefield, Mary E. Brown, Shirley Cavanaugh, James M. Kusack, Nolan Lushington, James Mullins, Elsie Okobi, and Josephine Sche.

PREFACE

Integrating music with other academic subjects is by no means a new idea. During the nineteenth century, for example, students routinely learned songs that purposefully reinforced lessons in science, mathematics, geography, history, and language arts. Educators of that time capitalized on the fact that a single song could captivate and motivate students, underscore a point, or make a lesson especially memorable. One of the best-known examples, and one that is still popular today, is the introduction of the alphabet to young children by singing the letters to the tune "Twinkle, Twinkle, Little Star." In the 1920s, and again in the 1960s, educators promoted an "interdisciplinary" model in which relationships between historical, scientific, and artistic subjects were emphasized. More recently, research in cognitive psychology has confirmed what many artists and some teachers have long recognized: There are "multiple intelligences" and different, but often mutually reinforcing, "ways of knowing" and learning. Today, more and more teachers are exploring different instructional approaches and tools, including music, to help students appreciate the real and significant connections that exist among the various fields of human endeavor. The purpose of this select guide is to help music specialists and nonspecialists identify resources that support the integration of music with core curriculum for kindergarten through eighth grade.

About the Guide

This guide is organized according to discipline—language arts, mathematics, science, and social studies. Topics are presented alphabetically within each subject area, with one exception: Topics in the American history section of the social studies chapter are presented in chronological order. For each topic, material is grouped according to format—Articles, Pamphlets, Books, and Recordings (LPs, audiocassettes, compact discs, and videocassettes). Additional material and information can be found in two groups that complete most topic sections—Further Sources of Songs and Further Reading. Further Sources of Songs generally consists of collections that contain relevant songs but provide little background information. Further Reading lists sources that may or may not contain songs or music but do offer extensive in-depth coverage of a particular topic. These works usually have been written by scholars with the academic community in mind. Cross-references, indicated by *See also* headings, follow each topic heading. A comprehensive subject index has been provided to locate specific topics more easily.

Items were selected for this guide based on content, quality, and grade level suitability. Another important evaluation criterion was orientation (practical or "how to" information rather than theoretical or "should do" information). Materials that provide practical applications—for example, lesson plans with the text and music—have been selected over those that simply present rationales for using music across the curriculum or in specific contexts. While a number of the resources given here are out of print, they are not necessarily "out of date." They contain valuable information and can often be found in school and public libraries.

Individual entries contain the following information: author(s), title, source, publisher, date of publication, number of pages, musical arrangement, paperback (if applicable), recording format (if applicable), grade suitability, and a brief descriptive annotation. Contact information has been provided for items that are available through private publishers or distributors. Accession numbers ("ED" followed by a six-digit number) are included for items available through ERIC.[1] Particularly noteworthy resources are indicated by an asterisk.

Below is a sample listing with a key to special entries that may appear.

Highly Recommended · Paperback · Grade Suitability · ERIC Number

3. *Scott, John Anthony, and Laurence I. Seidman. "Songs of the American Revolution, 1776-1777," *Folksong in the Classroom* 3, no. 1 (fall 1982): 6–26. (P.O. Box 925, Sturbridge, MA 01566) Arr. for guitar. [P] Grade 5+. [ED 391704]

A consistently excellent source of songs and information dedicated to enriching the study of social studies, literature, and the humanities (K–12) through the use of folksong, this issue offers 15 songs from the American Revolution with background notes as well as suggested activities and literature tie-ins. Songs include: "Young Ladies in Town"; "Liberty Song and a Parody, 1768"; "Castle Island Song"; "The Rich Old Lady"; "Fish and Tea"; "A Junto Song"; "Irishman's Epistle"; "The Deserter"; "British Grenadiers"; "Trip to Cambridge"; "Sir Peter Parker"; "Dying Redcoat"; and "Battle of Trenton."

Note

1. Sponsored by the US Department of Education, ERIC, or Educational Resource Information Center, is a clearinghouse for education-related material. Documents are submitted for inclusion, and those selected are either abstracted or copied in their entirety, given an accession number, and indexed. The regularly updated index is available in print, on CD-ROM, through online services, and via the Internet.

LANGUAGE ARTS

Language

♪ Books

1. *Mulligan, Mary Ann. *Integrating Music with Other Studies*. New York: Center for Applied Research in Education, 1975. (521 Fifth Avenue, New York, NY 10017) 64pp. [P] Grades 1–4.

   Published more than 20 years ago, this little booklet has more useful and practical ideas than many books ten times its size. The section on integrating music with language arts presents many activities that develop students' listening abilities and explore relationships between sounds and words.

2. Riley, Margaret C., and Donna L. Coe. *Whole Language: Discovery Activities for the Primary Grades*. West Nyack, NY: Center for Applied Research in Education, 1992. 323pp. Grades 1–4.

   Lesson plans for various activities that have language arts, science, mathematics, and social studies components are provided to "help teachers (and others) develop strategies and plan activities that actively engage children in language and literature." Units based on music and language center around the following songs: "I've Been Working on the Railroad"; "Polly Wolly Doodle"; "This Little Light of Mine"; "If You're Happy and You Know It"; "Magic Penny"; "Apples and Bananas"; "Over in the Meadow"; and "Jamaica Farewell."

Literature

 Book

3. *Levene, Donna B. *Music Through Children's Literature: Theme and Variations.* Englewood, CO: Teacher Ideas Press, 1993. 116pp. [P] Grades 1–6.

    Forty lesson plans explore the connections—rhythm, melody, form and style, instruments, dance and movement, and history—between children's literature and music. Each lesson is based on a specific children's book and includes a list of print and nonprint resources, key words, specific activities, presentation tips, and a follow-up.

 Further Reading

4. *Tooze, Ruth, and Beatrice Perham Krone. *Literature and Music As Resources for Social Studies.* Englewood Cliffs, NJ: Prentice-Hall, 1955. 457pp.

    Although some of the suggested children's books are out-of-date, this is a marvelous source of ideas for exploring the history of America and the cultures of other countries through children's literature and music. Specific books and songs (some with melodies) are provided throughout. Part I looks at the history of America and includes sections on African Americans, Native Americans, and various regional and ethnic groups. Part II explores the world through song and literature with special sections on Canada, Latin America, Europe, the Near East, Asia, Australia, and Africa.

Reading

 Book

5. List, Lynne K. *Music, Art and Drama Experiences for the Elementary Curriculum.* New York: Teachers College, Columbia University, 1982. 206pp. Grades 1–3.

    This book provides activities for integrating music with other core subjects. Chapter 3, "Reading Experiences," contains music activities that enhance word recognition, comprehension, vocabulary, and listening skills.

♪ *Further Source of Songs*

6. Reid, Rob. *Children's Jukebox: A Subject Guide to Musical Recordings and Programming Ideas for Songsters Ages 1 to 12.* Chicago: American Library Association, 1995. 225pp. Grades K–6.
    Arranged by subject, this select guide of 2,400 listings provides the titles for contemporary children's songs along with the performing artist, title of recording, publication date, and distributor. Titles are listed alphabetically within each subject. Brief annotations describe the songs and often include programming ideas. The section titled "Reading" is recommended, and the index is helpful.

Writing

Writing prose has much in common with writing music. . . . Every chapter, every paragraph, every sentence, I discovered, has an arc to it, like a musical phrase. Every word has both a meaning and a music.
■ Paul Fleischman, Newbery Award winner

♪ *Articles*

7. Cockburn, Victor. "The Uses of Folk Music and Songwriting in the Classroom," in *Arts As Education*, edited by Merryl Goldberg and Ann Phillips, 55-66. Cambridge, MA: *Harvard Educational Review*, 1992. Grades 1–4.
    Cockburn, a seasoned artist and educator who uses folk music to teach writing, describes specific techniques to help children explore the world of poetry and songwriting.

8. Kandall, Leslie. "We Write the Songs," *Teacher* 94 (February 1977): 100-104. Grades 1–3.
    This guide helps children improve penmanship, spelling, and reading skills through writing song lyrics.

9. Langfit, Diane. "Integrating Music, Reading, and Writing at the Primary Level," *The Reading Teacher* 47, no. 5 (February 1994): 430-31. Grades 1–4.
    Using common melodies, students develop writing and reading skills by writing songs about various topics. The author also suggests ways to use stories from children's literature for starting points and for follow-up activities.

4 / LANGUAGE ARTS

10. Ritz-Salmein, Dianne. "Music: Program Notes," *School Library Media Activities Monthly* XII, no. 4 (December 1995): 18–20. Grades 4+.

    This "how-to" guide helps students practice their writing skills by researching and writing program notes for a real or imaginary concert. A bibliography is included.

♪ Books

11. List, Lynne K. *Music, Art and Drama Experiences for the Elementary Curriculum.* New York: Teachers College, Columbia University, 1982. 206pp. Grades 1–3.

    This book provides many activities for integrating music with other core subjects. See Chapter 2, "Written Language Experiences," for music activities that enhance writing, spelling, and grammar.

12. *MacArthur, Margaret, with Gregory Sharrow. *The Vermont Heritage Songbook.* Middlebury, VT: The Vermont Folklife Center, 1994. 108pp. Arr. for guitar. [P] Accompanying cassette.

    A collection of 42 songs about people, events, and customs from Vermont, written by folklorist and folksong collector MacArthur in collaboration with school children from around the state who researched their town's local history. The introduction contains suggestions for integrating music into the regular curriculum. A topic index is included.

13. *Webber, Mary. *Writing Ballads from Local Historical Legends.* Yarmouth, MA: Yarmouth Historical Society, 1989. (P.O. Box 107, Yarmouth, MA 04096) 36pp. [P] Grades 3+.

    This excellent guide explains how to combine research in local history with ballad writing. Several well-known examples of historical ballads from literature are provided with grade appropriate suggestions on how to help students write their own songs.

MATHEMATICS

Mathematics is music for the mind; music is mathematics for the soul.
■ Anonymous

Mathematics is the arithmetic of sounds as optics is the geometry of light.
■ Claude Debussy

Mathematics and Music, the most sharply contrasted fields of intellectual activity which one can discover, and yet bound together, supporting one another as if they would demonstrate the hidden bond which draws together all activities of our mind, and which also in the revelations of artistic genius leads us to surmise unconscious expressions of a mysteriously active intelligence.
■ R. C. Archibald

I think there certainly is a link [between mathematics and music], for various reasons. One is that they are both creative arts. When you're sitting with a bit of paper creating mathematics, it is very like sitting with a sheet of music paper creating music. Both have rules which you must follow. They are also both languages. A page of mathematics and a page of music are both meaningless unless you happen to know what the various symbols mean and how they relate to each other. . . .
■ Robin Wilson, Mathematician

General

 Articles

14. Beyer, Jack, and Barbara Goy. "Oh Empty Set! Oh Empty Set! What If Music and Math Never Met?" *Music Educators Journal* 55 (September 1968): 63–69. Grades 5+.
    The creation of a short mathematics "operetta" on open sets is detailed in this article.

15. Moses, Barbara E., and Linda Proudfit. "Ideas," *Arithmetic Teacher* (December 1992): 215–18. Grades K–8.
    Focusing on the connection between mathematics and music, this resource provides lesson plans for classroom activities on topics such as rhythm and counting, fractions, time measurement, surveying techniques, and music preferences. Reproducible activity sheets are provided.

16. Rothenberg, Barbara Skolnick. "The Measure of Music," *Teaching Children Mathematics* (March 1996): 408–9. Grades K–6.
    Suggestions for combining songs and mathematics in weekly activities are presented in this article. Activities for grades kindergarten through two focus on patterns and measurement; those for grades three and four focus on measurement, fractions, and money; and those for grades five and six focus on monetary problem solving, area and perimeter, and fractions.

 Books

17. Garland, Trudi Hammel, and Charity Vaughan Kahn. *Math and Music: Harmonious Connections*. Palo Alto, CA: Dale Seymour Publications, 1995. 165pp. Grades 6+.
    In this book the authors demonstrate the close connection between music and mathematics while exploring proportion, patterns, Fibonacci numbers, the Golden Ratio, geometric transformations, trigonometric functions, fractals, and more. An explanation of how mathematics can be used to analyze musical rhythms, sound waves, tuning, and music composition is also included. A bibliography is provided.

18. *List, Lynne K. *Music, Art and Drama Experiences for the Elementary Curriculum.* New York: Teachers College, Columbia University, 1982. 206pp. Grades 1–3.

    This book provides suggested activities for integrating music with other core subjects. See Chapter 6, "Mathematics Experiences," for music activities that enhance knowledge and understanding of number facts, measuring time, and fractions.

19. Mendelsohn, Esther L. *Teaching Primary Math with Music: Grades K-3.* Palo Alto, CA: Dale Seymour Publications, 1990. 93pp. Arr. for piano. Accompanying cassette. [P] Grades K–3.

    Thirty songs composed by the author are offered that teach and review mathematics lessons on various topics—counting, addition, subtraction, early multiplication and division, telling time, money, beginning geometry, and measurement. Lesson plans and reproducible activity sheets are provided.

20. Mulligan, Mary Ann. *Integrating Music with Other Studies.* New York: Center for Applied Research in Education, 1975. (521 Fifth Avenue, New York, NY 10017) 64pp. [P] Grades 1–4.

    Published more than two decades ago, this little booklet is filled with superb ideas for integrating music with other disciplines. In the section on integrating music with mathematics, specific activities are provided for exploring the concept of sets, counting, comparing music and mathematics, and prediction and patterns.

Fractions
(*See also* Mathematics: General)

 Article

21. Godfrey, Margaret. "Fit Music into the Study of Fractions," *Teacher* 92, no. 8: 80–81. Grades 4–6.

    The focus of this article is the use of popular music and musical notation to reinforce skills involved in addition of fractions. A detailed sample lesson plan is given.

SCIENCE

Sure there is music even in the beauty, and the silent note which Cupid strikes, far sweeter than the sound of an instrument. For there is music wherever there is harmony, order and proportion; and thus far we may maintain the music of the spheres; for those well ordered motions, and regular paces, though they give no sound unto the ear, yet to the understanding they strike a note most full of harmony.

■ Religio Medici II, 9

General

 Book

22. *Mulligan, Mary Ann. *Integrating Music with Other Studies*. New York: Center for Applied Research in Education, 1975. (521 Fifth Avenue, New York, NY 10017) 64pp. [P] Grades 1–4.
      This small booklet is filled with superb ideas for integrating music with other disciplines, including science.

Animals

🎵 **Pamphlets**

23. Scott, John A., and Laurence I. Seidman. "Songs About Animals and Other Living Creatures," *Folksong in the Classroom* V, no. 3 (spring 1985): 59–75. (P.O. Box 925, Sturbridge, MA 01566) Arr. for guitar. Grades K–6.

  This resource provides songs and commentary to supplement stories about animals as well as a means to enrich discussions of conservation and ecology. Titles included are: "Aunt Rhody"; "Stewball"; "The Strawberry Roan"; "The Turtle Dove"; "The Mouse's Courting Song"; "The Blue Tail Fly"; "The Derby Ram"; and "The Ballad of the Boll Weevil." A bibliography of children's books about animals and a list of suggested activities are also included.

24. Scott, John W., John A. Scott, and Laurence Seidman. "Fowls of the Air: Wild and Domesticated," *Folksong in the Classroom* XII, no. 1 (fall 1991): 12–30. (P.O. Box 925, Sturbridge, MA 01566) Arr. for guitar. Grades 1–5.

  This resource, intended for social studies, humanities, and language arts teachers, contains the following songs: "I'll Give My Love a Cherry"; "Little Bird"; "The Cuckoo"; "The Lark in the Morning"; "The Three Ravens"; "The Grey Goose"; "Shule Aroon"; and "The Praties They Grow Small." It also includes suggested classroom activities and a bibliography.

 Recordings

25. *Animal Folk Songs for Children (and Other People)*. Performed by Mike and Peggy Seeger. Rounder Records, Cambridge, MA, 1992. audiocassette and compact disc, 58 min each.

  These recordings provide 58 American folksongs about all kinds of animals, including all of the songs in Ruth Crawford Seeger's book by the same title. Songs included are: "Little Brown Dog"; "Oh, Blue"; "Big Sheep (the Darby Ram)"; "Riding Round the Cattle"; "Old Cow Died"; "Raccoon and Possum"; "Cross-Eyed Gopher"; "Little Lap-Dog Lullaby"; "Jack, Can I Ride"; "Daddy Shot a Bear"; "Deer Song"; "And We Hunted and We Hunted"; "Mister Rabbit"; "Peep Squirrel"; "A Squirrel Is a Pretty Thing"; "Snake Baked a Hoecake"; "Old Lady Goose"; "My Hen's a Good Old Hen"; and "Of All the Beast-es."

26. *Birds, Beasts, Bugs and Little Fishes*. Performed by Pete Seeger. Smithsonian/Folkways 45021, Washington, DC. audiocassette. Grades K-4.

  Descriptive notes with lyrics are provided in this recording. Contents include: "Fly Through My Window"; "I Had a Rooster";

"Come All You Bold Sailormen"; "Old Grey Mule"; "Alligator, Hedgehog"; "Frog Went A-Courting"; "Raccoon's Got a Bushy Tail"; "I Know an Old Lady Who Swallowed a Fly"; "Ground Hog"; "Mister Rabbit"; "Grey Goose"; "Teency Weency Spider"; "The Old Hen"; "Skip To My Lou"; and "My Little Kitty."

27. *Lyrical Life Science.* Lyrical Learning, Corvallis, OR, 1995. (8008 Cardwell Hill, Corvallis, OR 97330) audiocassette, 29 min. Grades 6+.

Recognizing that rhyme and rhythm can help students remember specific information, this resource presents concepts and terminology from the life sciences set to music. Topics are: the scientific method, all living things, invertebrates, cold-blooded invertebrates, vertebrates, birds, plants, algae, viruses, and bacteria. A workbook and tests are also provided.

28. *Lyrical Life Science, Vol. 2—Mammals, Ecology, and Biomes.* Lyrical Learning, Corvallis, OR, 1996. (8008 Cardwell Hill, Corvallis, OR 97330) audiocassette, 44 min. Grades 4–6.

This recording makes a great deal of scientific information and terminology easier to remember by setting words and concepts to familiar melodies. A helpful teacher's guide is provided.

29. *Whale Watching.* Performed by Marylee Sunserl. Piper Grove Music, Pacific Grove, CA, 1994. (Box 1113, Pacific Grove, CA 93950) audiocassette, 35 min. Grades K–3.

Fourteen traditional and original songs about the seashore, the sea, and the animals that inhabit these ecosystems are presented.

♪ Further Sources of Songs

30. Reid, Rob. *Children's Jukebox: A Subject Guide to Musical Recordings and Programming Ideas for Songsters Ages 1 to 12.* Chicago: American Library Association, 1995. 225pp. Grades K–6.

Arranged by subject, this select guide provides the titles for contemporary children's songs along with the performing artist, title of recording, publication date, and distributor. Titles are listed alphabetically within each subject. Brief annotations describe each song and often give programming ideas. Subjects include animals, fish, birds, dogs, frogs, insects, and spiders. A good index is provided.

31. Seeger, Ruth Crawford. *Animal Folk Songs for Children.* Hamden, CT: Linnet Books, 1950, reprint 1993. 80pp. Grades K–4.

This classic collection contains 43 traditional American songs that feature animals. The songs are categorized by Woods and Field, Dogs and Hunting, and Farm and Ranch.

Environment

 ## Article

32. Masyga, Jean, and Gladys Van Alstine. "Birds, Waves, and Squeaky Grass," *Instructor* 83, no. 6 (February 1974): 66–68. Grades 1–6.

This article describes how to successfully combine listening activities, writing, poetry, and concern for the ecology with music. Students take outdoor walks; are introduced to topics of air, water, and soil pollution; and are then encouraged to compose ecology songs. The finished products of 11 students are shared.

 ## Pamphlets

33. *Project I-C-E, Music K-3, Environmental Education Guide*. Green Bay, WI: Wisconsin Department of Public Instruction, 1974. 47pp. Grades K–3. [ED 100693]

This music guide, the product of a joint effort of 235 classroom teachers from northeastern Wisconsin, promotes the use of music as an aid in developing awareness and understanding of environmental issues. Twelve minilesson plans offer multidisciplinary activities plus reference and resource materials for the following topics: the sun, the need for clean water, clean air, the ecosystem, plant growth, animals, plants and insects, and preservation. Included are the words and melodies to: "Bugs"; "Let's Keep Our World Clean"; "Over in the Meadow"; "Fog"; "Keep the World from Dying"; "Balance and Nature"; "Let It Be"; and "A Cricket in the Thicket."

34. *Project I-C-E, Music 4-6, Environmental Education Guide*. Green Bay, WI: Wisconsin Department of Public Instruction, 1974. 47pp. Grades 4–6. [ED 100694]

Based on the same premise as *Project I-C-E, Music K-3* (listed above), this guide is designed to develop environmental awareness in children, grades four through six. Twelve minilesson plans offer multidisciplinary activities plus reference and resource materials for the following topics: conservation and energy sources, clean air, clean water, pollution, overpopulation, ecosystems, man versus machine, land use, quality of life, and noise pollution. Included are the words and melodies for: "What Have They Done to the Rain?"; "Think About Your Troubles"; "My Dirty Stream"; "Litter Blows over the Highway"; "Pollution Ballad"; "A-Doublin'"; "Dry Bones"; "Ecology"; "Down with Pollution"; "John Henry"; "Leave Them a Flower"; "Oh, Cancerous"; "Gee I'm Looking Forward"; "Big Yellow Taxi"; "We Like It Here"; "Garbage"; and "Calico Cat."

35. Scott, John A., and Laurence I. Seidman. "Rivers of America, Part I & II," *Folksong in the Classroom* VII, no. 2 and 3 (winter/spring 1987): 42. (P.O. Box 925, Sturbridge, MA 01566) Arr. for guitar. Grades 5+. [ED 344784]

Folksong in the Classroom is a consistently excellent source of ideas and examples of using songs to teach topics in social studies and the humanities. Part I provides information and background material on using folk songs to examine the role of American rivers in economic life, transportation, national identity, exploration, settlement and urbanization, politics, and the lives of Native Americans. Part II explores issues related to ecology, natural resources, wildlife and science, literature, folklore and the arts, and the historical human tragedy associated with the use of rivers. Follow-up activities and a bibliography are provided.

Part I contains the following songs: "One More River"; "A La Claire Fontaine"; "Hudson River Steamboat"; "Banks of the Sacramento"; "Red River Valley"; "Banks of the Ohio"; "Coffee Grows on White Oak Trees"; "All Quiet on the Potomac"; and "No More Cane on the Brazos."

Part II's songs include: "My Bark Canoe"; "Death of General Wolfe"; "Ballad of Peter Gray"; "Lovely Ohio"; "Way Down Yonder in the Paw Paw Patch"; "We're Coming Arkansas"; "Down by the Riverside"; "Roll on Columbia"; and "My Dirty Stream."

36. *———. "Songs About Our Earth and Ecology: A Celebration of Nature and Its Defense," *Folksong in the Classroom* IX, no. 1 (fall 1988–winter/spring 1989): 9–12. [Part 1 of 3 parts]. (P.O. Box 925, Sturbridge, MA 01566) Arr. for guitar. Grades 4+. [ED310021]

This is the first of three issues devoted to the environment showing how songs help raise student awareness of the natural world, of the dangers that beset it, and of their own place in it. Along with an introduction and song notes, the following songs are given: "What Shall We Do When We All Go Out?"; "Home on the Range"; "Black Waters"; "Sweet Water Rolling"; "What Have They Done to the Rain?"; "Garbage"; "Who Has Seen the Wind?"; "God Bless the Grass"; and "Oh, Oh, the Sunshine." Also included in this issue is a brief article by Dave Orleans describing how to use music in environmental education. A bibliography and discography are provided.

 Recordings

37. *Earthy Songs. Performed by Ken Lonnquist. Aylmer Press, 1994. audiocassette, 59 min. Grades K–5.

Twenty-six environmental songs are performed, including "Water"; "Little Tree"; "You're a Rhino!"; "A Place in the Choir"; "Garbage"; "Whale Songs"; and "The Rainforests." Lyrics are provided.

14 / SCIENCE

38. *Let's Clean up Our Act: Songs for the Earth*. Performed by Tom Callinan and Ann Shapiro, 1989. audiocassette. (168 Shore Road, Clinton, CT 06413) Grades 4+.

    This cassette contains songs on such topics as pollution, ecology, conservation, and preservation. It contains the following songs: "Let's Clean up Our Act"; "Pollution"; "Garbage"; "You Can't Eat the Oysters"; "Habitat, Save What's Left"; "Who Dunnit"; "Who Will Tend My Garden"; "The Garden Song"; "Mother Ocean"; "Clouds"; and "This Land Is Your Land."

39. *Mother Earth*. Performed by Tom Chapin. A & M Records, 1994. audiocassette. Grades 2–6.

    Contemporary songs about ecology are the focus of this recording. Titles included are: "A Song of One"; "Two Kinds of Seagulls"; "The Wheel of the Water"; "The Picnic of the World"; "Sailing to the Sea"; "Good Garbage"; "Mother Earth's Routine"; "Cousins"; "On My Way to School"; "Stone Soup"; "A Capital Ship"; "All Through the Night"; and "Thanksgiving Day."

40. *Nature Nuts*. Berkeley, CA: Song Trek, 1991. (2600 Hillagrass, Berkeley, CA 94704) audiocassette. Grades 1–6.

    The first side of this recording contains a collection of songs about nature and ecology. The second side showcases songs about pollution and solutions to environmental problems. Titles performed include: "All God's Critters"; "Romp in the Swamp"; "Hey, Ms. Spider"; "Camp Granada"; "Mud, Mud, Mud"; "Bats Eat Bugs"; "Newts, Salamanders and Frogs"; "Nature's Niches"; "Go into the Night"; "Pollution"; "Garbage Men Blues"; "Dirt"; "Garbage Blues"; "Packin' for My Hike"; "Hey, Hey, Don't Throw It Away"; "Working Together in the Sun"; "Garbage"; and "Ally Ally Oxen Free."

41. *Piggyback Planet: Songs for a Whole Earth*. Performed by Sally Rogers. Round River Records 301. (Available from Alcazar Records, P.O. Box 429, South Main St., Waterbury, VT 05676) audiocassette and compact disc. Grades 2–6.

    This recording features songs that emphasize environmental protection and conservation, and it includes these songs: "Garbage"; "Junk Round"; "The Planet Recycle Song"; "I Walk in Beauty"; "What Did the Dinosaurs Say?"; "This Land Is Your Land"; "Hello Lady Bug"; "Over in the Endangered Meadow"; "Rain Round"; "What Have They Done to the Rain?"; "K'ang Ting Song"; "La Tierraes Mi Madre"; and "Whale Song."

42. *Two Hands Hold the Earth*. Performed by Sarah Pirtle. Albany, NY: Gentle Wind 1028, 1984. (Available from A Gentle Wind, Box 3103, Albany, NY 12203) audiocassette, 40 min. Grades 1–5.

Songs and stories about nature, ecology, and conservation are performed in this recording. Titles include: "The Magic Horse"; "The Fox's Dance"; "Pelorus Jack"; "May There Always Be Sunshine"; "Across the Wide Ocean"; "My Roots Go Down"; "The Woman Who Gobbled Swiss Cheese"; "There's Always Something You Can Do"; "Wish I Was a Whale"; "Two Hands Hold the Earth"; "De Colores"; "That Quiet Place"; "Races"; "Brother Possum"; "I Talk to My Food"; "I Am a Person"; "Here's a Hand"; and "The Moon's Lullaby."

 Further Sources of Songs

43. DiSavino, Liza, ed. *For the Beauty of the Earth*. Mendham, NJ: The Folk Project, 1993. 107 pp. (Available from Hudson River Sloop Clearwater, 112 Market St., Poughkeepsie, NY 12601) Arr. for guitar. [P]
   More than 70 contemporary environmental and nature songs are given here and are listed in an index with suggested grade levels.

44. Reid, Rob. *Children's Jukebox: A Subject Guide to Musical Recordings and Programming Ideas for Songsters Ages 1 to 12*. Chicago: American Library Association, 1995. 225pp.
   Arranged by subject, this select guide provides the titles for contemporary children's songs, along with the performing artist, title of recording, publication date, and distributor. Titles are listed alphabetically within each subject. Brief annotations describe the song and often include programming ideas. The "Ecology" and "Earth" sections are recommended, and a good index is provided.

Physics

Sound

 Article

45. "The Beat of the Band," *Science and Children* 23, no. 3 (November/December 1985): 32–33. Grades 1–4.
   This article offers activities to help students see, feel, and hear vibrations and better understand their relationship to sound. It also gives suggestions for making simple instruments—drums, kazoos, rubber band banjos, rubber hose horns, and tambourines—out of household objects.

Book

46. List, Lynne K. *Music, Art and Drama Experiences for the Elementary Curriculum.* New York: Teachers College, Columbia University, 1982. 206pp. Grades 1–3.
    This book provides many activities for integrating music with other core subjects. See Chapter 5, "Science Experiences," for music activities that enhance the knowledge and understanding of sound.

 Recordings

47. *The Clarinet, the Washtub, and the Musical Nails: How Musical Instruments Work.* (Blue Sky Associates, P.O. Box 349, Winchester, MA) videocassette, 59 min. Grades 7+.
    In this video, Robert Greenler gives a highly entertaining and informative physics lecture. Using soda bottles, wine glasses, metal bars, and toys, he explains the properties of vibrating strings, air columns, and solids. The lecture ends with thoughtful comments on the connections among art, music, poetry, and science.

48. *Science and Music.* Princeton, NJ: Films for the Humanities & Sciences, 1990. 5 videocassettes, 310 min. Grades 6+.
    In this series of videos, Charles Taylor gives lectures and demonstrations on music, sound waves, and acoustics. Titles in this five-part series include: "What Is Music?"; "The Essence of Instruments"; "Science, Strings, and Symphonies"; "Technology, Trumpets, and Tunes"; and "Scales, Synthesizers, and Samplers."

Plants

 Article

49. Clark, Elizabeth. "The Seed That Grew," *Instructor* (March 1961): 59–61.
    The author describes a successful third-grade learning activity on plant growth in which a play was produced, complete with costumes, creative dancing, and original songs.

Further Source of Songs

50. Reid, Rob. *Children's Jukebox: A Subject Guide to Musical Recordings and Programming Ideas for Songsters Ages 1 to 12.* Chicago: American Library Association, 1995. 225pp.

    Arranged by subject, this guide provides the titles for contemporary children's songs along with the performing artist, title of recording, publication date, and distributor. Titles are listed alphabetically within each subject. Brief annotations describe the song and often include programming ideas. Recommended sections are "Plants," "Garden," and "Farms." A helpful index is included.

Technology

Instrument Building

 Articles

51. "The Beat of the Band," *Science and Children* 23, no. 3 (November/December 1985): 32-33. Grades 1–4.

    This article presents activities to help young students see, feel, and hear vibrations and understand their relationship to sound. Included are suggestions for making simple instruments—drums, kazoos, rubber band banjos, rubber hose horns, and tambourines—out of household objects.

52. Cline, Dallas. "Making Simple Folk Instruments for Children," *Music Educators Journal* 66 (February 1980): 50–53.

    This article discusses construction of several simple folk instruments and offers activity suggestions.

 Books

53. Britsch, Barbara M., and Amy Dennison-Tansey. *One Voice: Music and Stories in the Classroom.* Englewood, CO: Teacher Ideas Press, 1995. 175pp. Grades 1–4.

    Lesson plans are given for making the following instruments: musical streamers, shaker cups, rhythm sticks, guiros, sandpaper blocks, panpipes, xylophones, tubular bells, and bullroarers.

54. Cline, Dallas. *Homemade Instruments*. New York: Oak Publications, 1976. (Originally published under the title *Cornstalk Fiddle and Other Homemade Instruments*) 26pp. Grades 4+.

Cline shows how to make 30 folk instruments from easy-to-find materials and includes music and lyrics to a number of fun folksongs.

55. Hunter, Ilene, and Marilyn Judson. *Simple Folk Instruments to Make and Play*. New York: Simon and Schuster, 1977. 159pp. Grades 4+.

The authors demonstrate through text and pictures how to make more than 100 instruments, often with materials that can easily be found at home. Instruments are divided into percussion, string, and wind types and include drums, rattles, banjos, zithers such as dulcimers, flutes, whistles, and horns. Each section ends with a "Quick and Simple" page with suggestions for making simplified versions of the instruments in just minutes. An introductory section provides suggestions for using the instruments in conjunction with other areas of study as well as tips on working with various materials.

 Recordings

56. *Making and Playing Homemade Musical Instruments*. Kathy Fink and Marcie Marxer. Homespun Video, 1989. videocassette, 65 min. Grades 1–6.

Fink and Marxer demonstrate how to make and play the yardstick mouthbow, oatmeal box conga drums, bleach-bottle banjos, bottle cap castanets, tin can maracas, the spoons, washboards, and the washtub bass.

57. *My First Music Video: A Kids' Guide for Fun to Make Musical Instruments*. Sony Kids' Video, 1993. videocassette, 50 min. Grades 3–6.

This video gives students step-by-step instructions on how to make their own musical instruments—xylophone, tom-tom, bells, rattles, tambourine, banjo, and others. Instructions for playing each instrument are given and demonstrated.

SOCIAL STUDIES

Songs are a statement of a people. You can learn more about people by listening to their songs than any other way, for into songs go all the hopes and hurts, the angers, fears, wants and aspirations.
■ John Steinbeck

African Americans
(See also American History: Civil Rights Movement, Civil War, General, Slavery)

 *Articles*

58. Campbell, Patricia Shehan. "Mellonee Burnim on African American Music," *Music Educators Journal* (1995): 41–49. Grades 4+.
    In this interview, a noted ethnomusicologist discusses the history and characteristics of gospel music. Suggested activities are presented as well as a bibliography.

59. *Reagon, Bernice Johnson, and Luvenia A. George. "Teaching the Music of African Americans," in *Teaching Music with a Multicultural Approach*, edited by William M. Anderson, 11–21. Reston, VA: Music Educators National Conference, 1991. Grades 6+.
    Two authorities on African American music present information on the importance of African American religious traditions, particularly in spiritual and gospel music. A lesson plan to help students recognize the unique characteristics of spirituals is provided and includes the following songs: "Going to Shout All over God's Heav'n"; "Ev'ry Time I Feel the Spirit"; "Git on Board Little Children"; "We'll Understand It Better By and By"; "Heavenly Sunshine"; and "Praise the Lord." A bibliography and discography are provided.

20 / SOCIAL STUDIES

60. *Standifer, James A. "African Americans," in *Multicultural Perspectives in Music Education*, edited by William M. Anderson and Patricia Shehan Campbell, 48–67. Reston, VA: Music Educators National Conference, 1989. Grades 6+.

This chapter provides an excellent introduction to the music of African Americans as well as detailed lesson plans with support material. The lessons explore variations of melodic lines, call and response types of songs, the blues, ragtime, spirituals, and jazz. A bibliography, discography, and filmography are included.

 Books

61. Glass, Paul. *Songs and Stories of Afro-Americans*. New York: Grosset & Dunlap, 1971. 161pp. Grades 7+.

Twenty-one songs are presented here, including sections on Duke Ellington, W. C. Handy, Leadbelly, and others.

62. *Silverman, Jerry. *Just Listen to This Song I'm Singing: African American History Through Song*. Brookfield, CT: Millbrook, 1996. 95pp. Arr. for piano and guitar. [P] Grades 4+.

Silverman, a prolific compiler of folksong anthologies, presents 13 songs from the African American tradition. A helpful introduction and explanatory notes are included.

 Recordings

63. *American Patchwork: The Land Where the Blues Began*. PBS, 1990. (Home Video 260, Beverly Hills, CA. Distributed by Pacific Arts) videocassette, 60 min., color. Grades 8+.

This video traces the development of the delta blues, including the connection with Africa, worship songs, and the work songs of mule skinners, river roustabouts, sharecroppers, and prisoners.

64. *The Black Experience As Expressed Through Music*. Los Angeles Public Schools, Music Division, Los Angeles, 1978. (Available from Beem Foundation, 3864 Grayburn Ave., Los Angeles, CA 90008) 4 videocassettes, 60 min. each.

Topics covered on these videos include gospel, spirituals, jazz, and ragtime as well as an interview with Eubie Blake.

65. *Discovering Jazz*. AMS Media (9710 De Soto Ave., Chatsworth, CA 91311-4409) videocassette, 21 min., color. Grades 3–6.

This video presents various styles of jazz, including dixieland, blues, swing, bop, cool, and funk. A jazz session that includes improvisation with electronic resources concludes the performance.

66. *Echoes of America*. Landmark Film, Falls Church, VA, 1991. videocassette, 52 min.
>This video focuses on the banjo and its introduction to America by African slaves and the development of various playing styles. Musicians Odell Thompson, Bill Munroe, Bill Keith, and Pete Seeger are featured.

67. *Teaching the Music of African Americans*. Reston, VA: Music Educators National Conference, 1991. Videocassette, 25 min. color.
>Bernice Johnson Reagon and Luvenia A. George discuss the roots of African American music with particular emphasis on the role of religion in music. Performances by and an interview with Daniel E. Sheehy about Afro-Cuban music is included.

68. **Tryin' to Get Home: A History of African-American Song*. Heebie Jeebie Music, Berkeley, CA, 1993. (1608 Julia Street, Berkeley, CA 94703-2018) videocassette, 60 min.
>Combining narration and song, this video explores various aspects of African American song, including examples of children's game songs, spirituals, folksongs, minstrel songs, Broadway songs, early rock 'n' roll, Motown, gospel, and rap.

♪ Further Sources of Songs

69. *Jones, Bessie, and Bess Lomax Hawes. *Step It Down: Games, Plays, Songs, and Stories from the Afro-American Heritage*. New York: Harper and Row, 1972. (Accompanying recording available from Rounder Records #8004, 1 Camp Street, Cambridge, MA 02140) Grades 3–6.
>The subtitle tells it all: "Games, Plays, Songs, and Stories from the Afro-American Heritage."

70. Lomax, Alan. *Folk Songs of North America*. New York: Doubleday, 1960. 623pp. Arr. for banjo and guitar. [P]
>Eighty-two songs by one of America's foremost authorities on folksongs are presented here, including spirituals, work songs, ballads, and blues.

71. Silverman, Jerry. *Work Songs*. Broomall, PA: Chelsea,1994. 64pp. Arr. for piano and guitar. [P] Grades 4+.
>This book includes 29 songs from or about African American folk workers.

Further Reading

72. Courlander, Harold. *Negro Folk Music, U.S.A.* New York: Columbia University Press, 1963. 324pp.
    Courlander explores the development of vocal and instrumental African American music. Included are discussions and examples of song-games, spirituals, slave songs, blues, and gospel. A bibliography and discography are provided.

73. George, Luvenia A. "The Source of African-American Music," in *Teaching Music with a Multicultural Approach*, edited by William M. Anderson, 6–10. Reston, VA: Music Educators National Conference, 1991.
    Luvenia, a noted ethnomusicologist, gives a comprehensive overview of the history of African American music, from spirituals to gospel music.

74. Greenway, John. *American Folksongs of Protest*. Philadelphia: University of Pennsylvania Press, 1953, reprint 1960. 348pp.
    The history of protest song in America is divided into chapters on songs of African Americans, textile workers, miners, migrant workers, farmers, and others. See the chapter titled "Negro Songs of Protest" for a good discussion on slave songs and more. A discography and bibliography are included.

75. *Jones, Arthur C. *Wade in the Water: The Wisdom of the Spirituals*. Maryknoll, NY: Orbis Books, 1993. 182pp.
    This book provides an excellent review of the literature and an analysis of spirituals, including their development, meaning, and use from slave times to the present, particularly in reference to their psychological importance.

76. *Southern, Eileen. *The Music of Black Americans: A History*. 1977. Reprint, New York: W. W. Norton, 1983. 552pp. [P]
    This is the standard work on Afro-American music, covering all aspects of African American music from its African roots to the mid-twentieth century. A bibliography and discography are included.

77. Titon, Jeff Todd. "Music of Worship, Music of Work, Music of Play: The Blues," in *Worlds of Music: An Introduction to the Music of the World's Peoples*, edited by Jeff Todd Titon, James T. Koetting, David P. McAllester, David B. Reck, and Mark Slobin. New York: Schirmer Books, 1984. 105–65.
    Titon provides a good introduction to the blues, including its history, character, and meaning. Titon gives an account of the life of Lazy Bill Lucas and provides plans for making a one-stringed diddly-bow. A bibliography and discography are provided.

American History

General

 *Article*

78. Daniels, Elva S. "America in Song," *Instructor* 85, no. 2 (October 1975): 72-94. Grades 1-6.
    This article presents a sampling of folksongs that illustrate various topics and eras in American history. Words, usually for first verse and chorus only, are presented for the following songs: (Revolution) "Liberty Song"; "Chester"; "Goody Bull"; and "The World Turned Upside Down"; (Expanding Frontier) "No Hidin' Place"; "Lazy John"; "Shenandoah"; and "When I Went Off to Prospect"; (Civil War) "Tenting Tonight"; (Settlers & Workers) "Paddy on the Railroad"; "Little Old Sod Shanty"; and "Lumberjack's Song"; (War and Depression) "I Don't Want Your Millions, Mister"; (1960s) "We Shall Overcome"; "Little Boxes"; "Waist Deep in the Big Muddy"; and "Blowin' in the Wind."

 Pamphlet

79. *Daly, Cindy L. *Integrating Social Studies and Folk Music: Resource Guide 3*. Albany, NY: New York State Department of Education, 1987. 73pp. [P] [ED 287784]
    This is a superb resource that includes a good introduction on folk music, suggestions for integrating social studies and folk music concepts, and learning activities. Instructional units include: What Is Folk Music?; Instruments; Folksongs as History; Singing About Jobs; and Expressing Feelings in Music. Suggestions for hiring a performing artist as well as a bibliography and a media listing are included.

 Books

80. Ives, Burl. *The Burl Ives Song Book: American Song in Historical Perspective*. New York: Ballantine Books, 1953. 275pp. Arr. for guitar. [P] Grades 1-6.
    Along with a successful career in acting, Ives was also well known for his performance of folksongs. Here he presents 115 songs that reflect U.S. history and heritage.

81. *Scott, John Anthony. *The Ballad of America: The History of the United States in Song and Story.* 1966. Reprint, Carbondale, IL: Southern Illinois University Press, 1983. 439pp. Arr. for guitar. [P] Grades 5+.

Scott, an educator and longtime advocate for the use of primary sources in the teaching of social studies and the humanities, has put together an outstanding resource for teachers. This collection of 125 songs, with excellent chapter and introductory song notes, tells the story of America from the first settlements to modern times. Chapters include: The Colonial Period (British Heritage, Colonial Songs, and Ballads); The American Revolution; The Early National Period; Jacksonian America (Sea and Immigration, Westward Movement, and Slavery Days); The Civil War; Between the Civil War and the First World War (Farmers, Immigrants, and the Negro People); Between the Two World Wars; and Since the War. An afterword explores the significant role that folksongs can play in K-12 classrooms. A bibliography and discography are provided.

82. Silverman, Jerry. *Mel Bay Presents the American History Songbook.* Pacific, MO: Mel Bay Publications, 1992. 231pp. Arr. for piano and guitar. [P] Grades 4+.

This anthology presents 80 songs ranging from the Colonial period to the Vietnam War as well as songs from various movements such as the abolitionist, labor rights, civil rights, and women's rights. Brief song notes are included.

83. *Tooze, Ruth, and Beatrice Perham Krone. *Literature and Music As Resources for Social Studies.* Englewood Cliffs, NJ: Prentice-Hall, 1955. 457pp.

Although some of the suggested children's books are out-of-date, this is still a marvelous source of ideas for exploring the history of America through children's literature and music. Specific books and songs (some with melodies) are provided. Divided into several parts, Part I looks at the history of America and includes sections on Blacks, Native Americans, and various regional and ethnic groups. Bibliographies are included.

 Recordings

84. *American History in Ballad and Song.* Performed by various artists. vols. 1 and 2. Smithsonian/Folkways 5801 and 5802, Washington, DC. audiocassette and compact disc. Grades 5+.

This is a compilation of songs drawn from other Smithsonian/Folkways recordings by artists such as Pete Seeger, Cisco Houston, Oscar Brand, and others. The emphasis is on revolution, westward expansion, the Civil War, and labor. Descriptive background notes on songs, lyrics, and classroom activities are provided. Titles include: "Washer Lad"; "Shamrock"; "When I Was Single"; "Ballad of the

Tea Party"; "Liberty Song"; "Dying Sergeant"; "Battle of Saratoga"; "Cornwallis Burgoyned"; "Buffalo Skinners"; "Davy Crockett"; "Sioux Indians"; "Greer County Bachelor"; "Crossing the Plains"; "Cowboy Yodel"; "Free Elections"; "Jefferson and Liberty"; "Andrew Jackson"; "Oh Dear, What Can the Matter Be?"; "No Irish Need Apply"; "Harrison Song"; "Hail, Africa Band"; "Abolitionist Hymn"; "Bonnie Blue Flag"; "*Cumberland* Crew"; "General Patterson"; "In Charleston Jail"; "All Quiet Along the Potomac"; "Lincoln and Liberty"; "Old Rebel"; "Pittsburg Town"; "Blind Fiddler"; "Dust Storm Disaster"; "Eight Hour Day"; and "My Children Are Seven in Number."

85. *Insights into American History Through Folk Songs*. Performed by Keith McNeil and Rusty McNeil. WEM Records, 1989. (16230 Van Buren Boulevard, Riverside, CA 92504) 6 sets: 2 cassettes each. audiocassette and compact disc. Grades 4+.

Folksongs from different periods of American history—from the colonial period to the Great Depression—are performed here. Titles of sets include: "Colonial and Revolution Songs"; "Moving West Songs"; "Civil War Songs"; "Cowboy Songs"; "Western Railroad Songs"; and "Working and Union Songs." For specific titles in each set, see individual topics.

86. *The Musical Heritage of America*. Performed by Tom Glazer. 3 vols. CMS 650. New York: CMS Records, 1972–1974. LP and audiocassette. Grades 4+.

This recording contains narration and songs along with a study guide providing the narration script and song lyrics.

Volume I, *From Colonial Times to the Beginning of the Civil War* (4 cassettes), includes: "Who Is the Man?"; "When Jesus Wept"; "Tobacco's But an Indian Weed"; "Little Mohee"; "Indian Christmas Carol"; "House Carpenter"; "Lord Rendal"; "Barbara Allen"; "Pretty Polly"; "Springfield Mountain"; "Paper of Pins"; "Henry Martin"; "Golden Vanity"; "Blow Ye Winds"; "Brave Wolfe"; "What a Court Hath Old England"; "Chester"; "Riflemen of Bennington"; "Battle Song of Saratoga"; "Boston Tea Tax"; "Liberty Song"; "Paul Jones' Victory"; "Johnny Has Gone for a Soldier"; "Captain Kidd"; "Pirate Song"; "High Barbaree"; "Blow the Man Down"; "Haul Away, Joe"; "*Constitution* and the *Guerrière*"; "Hornet and the Peacock"; "Ye Parliaments of England"; "Hunters of Kentucky"; "Cumberland Gap"; "Peter Gray"; "Sweet Betsy from Pike"; "On the Banks of the Ohio"; "Blue-Tail Fly"; "O Susannah"; "Wayfaring Stranger"; "Farmer's Cursed Wife"; "Go Tell Aunt Rhody"; "Old Blue"; "Shenando"; "The Whale"; "ERIE"; "Got an Old Mule"; "Old Dan Tucker"; "Sourwood Mountain"; "Lolly Toodum"; "Pat Works on the Railway"; "Careless Love"; "Down in the Valley"; "Turkey in the Straw"; "Buffalo Gals"; "In the Days of Forty-Nine"; and "Sacramento."

Volume II, *The Civil War* (4 cassettes) contains the titles: "I Am Sold and Going to Georgia"; "Run to Jesus"; "Johnny, Won't You

Ramble"; "Follow the Drinking Gourd"; "Oh, Freedom"; "Bright Sparkles"; "Aura Lea"; "John Brown's Body"; "Battle Hymn of the Republic"; "Dixie"; "Maryland, My Maryland"; "Yellow Rose of Texas"; "Bonnie Blue Flag"; "Battle Cry of Freedom"; "Wait for the Wagon"; "Raw Recruit"; "We Are Coming, Father Abraham"; "Upidee Song"; "Lorena"; "Goober Peas"; "Army Bean"; "All Quiet Along the Potomac"; "Tenting on the Old Camp Ground"; "Just Before the Battle, Mother"; "Weeping, Sad and Lonely"; "Tramp, Tramp, Tramp"; "Vacant Chair"; "Treasury Rats"; "Year of Jubilo"; "Wake Nicodemus"; "Marching Through Georgia"; "When Johnny Comes Marching Home"; "Cumberland's Crew"; "Hold the Fort"; "In Charleston Jail"; "General Patterson"; "For Bales"; "Cumberland Gap"; "Unreconstructed Rebel"; "Wearing of the Grey"; "Conquered Banner"; and "President's Grave."

Volume III, *The Winning of the West* (4 LPs) includes: "Great Granddad"; "Sherman Cyclone"; "Common Bill"; "Lane County Bachelor"; "Housewife's Lament"; "Home on the Range"; "Old Settler's Song"; "I Ride an Old Paint"; "Git Along Little Dogies"; "Old Chisholm Trail"; "Sioux Indians"; "Streets of Laredo"; "Custer's Last Charge"; "Frankie and Johnny"; "Roving Gambler"; "Jesse James"; "Duncan and Brady"; "Sam Bass"; "In the Days of 49"; "Sacramento"; "Clementine"; "Pike County Miner"; "Sweet Betsy from Pike"; "He's the Man for Me"; "Pat Works on the Railway"; "Casey Jones"; "She'll Be Coming Round the Mountain"; "Midnight Special"; "John Henry"; "Hallelujah I'm a Bum"; "Jam on Gerry's Rocks"; "On the Banks of the Little Eau Pleine"; "Frozen Logger"; "River in the Pines"; "Flat River Girl"; "I Wish I Was Single Again"; "Raise a Ruckus"; "Oh, Susannah"; "Old Dan Tucker"; "Blue-Tail Fly"; "Green Grow the Lilacs"; "Have You Struck Ile"; "Little Old Sod Shanty"; "Elanoy"; "Dakota Land"; and "Buffalo Skinners."

87. *Voices of American History*. By Steven Traugh. 3 vols. Cypress, CA: Creative Teaching Press, 1994. audiocassette. Grades 3–6.

Three sets are included in this recording, each with 38- to 40-page booklets containing narratives, lyrics, activities, and performance tips. Songs with narrative are on one side of the tape, with music only on the other for class/assembly performance accompaniment.

Volume I, *Pre-Colonial Through the Revolutionary War*, includes the titles: "Mountain Hymn"; "I'm Going to A-meri-cay"; "My Bonnie Lies over the Ocean"; "When I First Came to This Land"; "The Greenland Whale"; "The Distressed Damsel"; "Nobody Knows the Trouble I've Seen"; "Green Grass Grows All Around"; "British Grenadiers"; "Revolutionary Tea"; "Free America"; "Revolutionary War Medley" ("Yankee Doodle," "Song of the Minutemen," "Yankee Privateer," "Johnny Has Gone for a Soldier," "Old Soldiers of the King," "World Turned Upside Down"); and "Hail Columbia."

Volume II, *The Young Nation Through the Civil War*, contains the titles: "Green Corn"; "America"; "Flag of the Brave and the Free"; "Songs of Everyday Life Medley" ("Turkey in the Straw," "Boil Them Cabbage Down," "Pick a Bale of Cotton," "Hush Little Baby"); "Peg and Awl"; "Four Pence a Day"; "Ye Parliament of England"; "Erie Canal"; "Follow the Drinkin' Gourd"; "Civil War Medley" ("Lincoln and Liberty," "Bonnie Blue Flag," "Eating Goober Peas," "Just Before the Battle," "Mother," "Slavery Chain Done Broke at Last"); and "Victory Song of Freedom."

Volume III, *Westward Expansion of the United States*, includes: "Cumberland Gap"; "Lovely Ohio"; "To the West"; "Shenandoah"; "Texas and Mexican War Medley" ("Cielito Lindo," "Remember the Alamo"); "Sweet Betsy from Pike"; "California Gold Rush Medley" ("Oh, California," "A Chinese-American Doodle"); "Starving to Death on a Government Claim"; "Jam on Jerry's Rock"; "Drill Ye Tarriers", "Drill"; "Little Bighorn"; "Old Chisholm Trail"; and "America the Beautiful."

 Further Sources of Songs

88. Arnett, Hazel. *I Hear America Singing! Great Folk Songs from the Revolution to Rock*. New York: Praeger Publications, 1975. 226 pp. Arr. for piano and guitar.

One hundred songs arranged chronologically are offered in this book, along with a brief synopsis of American and music history for each period. Notes on individual songs are not included.

89. Lomax, John A., and Alan Lomax. *Folk Song, U.S.A.* New York: Signet Books, 1966. 512pp. Arr. for piano and guitar. [P]

This is a collection of 111 songs by two of the foremost authorities on American folk music. Categories include songs about animals, love, the southern mountains, soldiers, sailors, lumbering, cowboys, farmers, trains, heroes and outlaws, and African Americans. An annotated bibliography and a discography are provided.

90. Sandburg, Carl. *The American Songbag*. 1927. Reprint, San Diego, CA: Harcourt Brace, 1990. 528pp. Arr. for piano.

Sandburg had an abiding love of American folksongs, often performing them as part of his lectures and readings. Here he has gathered 280 songs and provided interesting notes. Sections include pioneer songs, work songs, and songs from various regions.

Further Reading

91. Farucci, Samuel L. *A Folk Song History of America: America Through Its Songs*. Englewood Cliffs, NJ: Prentice Hall, 1984. 260pp.

This primer emphasizes important aspects of American folksong and provides short examples from different periods in American history. Topics include: description of folksong, characteristics of American folksong, songs from the Revolution, folksongs from the southern mountains, westward movement songs, African American songs, sailor songs, songs of the Civil War, cowboy songs, the railroad in folksong, the Gay '90s, the folksong revival, and urban folksongs.

92. Lawrence, Vera Brodsky. *Music for Patriots, Politicians, and Presidents: Harmonies and Discords of the First Hundred Years*. New York: Macmillan, 1975. 480pp.

In this handsome collection of broadsides and sheet music, Lawrence traces the political history of America. Each song, many of which are facsimile reproductions of the original source, is accompanied by an informative commentary.

Colonial Period

(*See also* American History: General)

 Pamphlet

93. *Scott, John Anthony, and Laurence I. Seidman. "Folk Songs of Colonial Times," *Folksong in the Classroom* I, no. 3 (February 1981): 22. (P.O. Box 925, Sturbridge, MA 01566) Arr. for guitar. Grades 5+.

Designed by teachers, this publication is an excellent source for units on American history through songs. Published three to four times a year, each issue gives a good overview of a particular topic, a number of songs with background notes, follow-up activities, and more. The colonial period is the focus of this issue. Songs include: "The Sycamore Tree"; "The Old Man Who Lived in the Woods"; "Let's Go a-Hunting"; "A Paper of Pins"; "Deirin Dé"; "Soldier, Soldier, Will You Marry Me?"; "The Fox;" and "Father Abby's Will."

 Recordings

94. *Colonial and Revolution Songs*. Performed by Keith McNeil and Rusty McNeil. WEM Records. (16230 Van Buren Boulevard, Riverside, CA 92504) audiocassette and compact disc, 120 min. Grades 4+.

Forty songs with narration are presented on two cassettes. Parts I and II cover seventeenth- and eighteenth-century America;

part III covers the American Revolution; part IV covers the War of 1812. Titles include: "The Girl I Left Behind Me"; "*The Golden Vanity*"; "We Gather Together"; "Old Hundred"; "The Willow Tree"; "The Great Silkie of Shule Skerry"; "Jennie Jenkins"; "The Trappan'd Maiden"; "When I First Came to This Land"; "The Sheepstealer"; "Soldier, Soldier Will You Marry Me?"; "Devil's Dream"; "Red-Haired Boy"; "Whiskey in the Jar"; "Kugadza Umambo"; "Michael Row the Boat Ashore"; "Jubal"; "The Mist Covered Mountain"; "Mouth Music"; "The Hoosier"; "The Greenland Whale Fishery"; "The Death of General Wolfe"; "British Grenadiers"; "Free America"; "Castle Island Song"; "Rich Lady over the Sea"; "Yankee Doodle"; "Battle of the Kegs"; "Chester"; "Johnny Has Gone for a Soldier"; "The World Turned Upside Down"; "Hail Columbia"; "The Eighth of January"; "Sinclair's Defeat"; "Parliament of England"; "Noble Lads of Canada"; "The *Constitution* and the *Guerrière*"; "To Anacreon in Heaven"; "Patriotic Diggers"; and "Hunters of Kentucky." The set comes with an accompanying songbook.

95. *Voices of American History: Vol. I, Pre-Colonial Through the Revolutionary War*. By Steven Traugh. Cypress, CA: Creative Teaching Press, 1994. audiocassettes. Grades 3–6.

This collection comes with a 38-page booklet that contains narratives, lyrics, activities, and performance tips. Songs and narratives are found on the first tape. The second tape is strictly music for class performances. Titles include: "Mountain Hymn"; "I'm Going to A-meri-cay"; "My Bonnie Lies over the Ocean"; "When I First Came to This Land"; "The Greenland Whale"; "The Distressed Damsel"; "Nobody Knows the Trouble I've Seen"; "Green Grass Grows All Around"; "British Grenadiers"; "Revolutionary Tea"; "Free America"; "Revolutionary War Medley" ("Yankee Doodle," "Song of the Minutemen," "Yankee Privateer," "Johnny Has Gone for a Soldier," "Old Soldiers of the King," "World Turned Upside Down"); and "Hail Columbia."

 Further Source of Songs

96. Vinson, Lee. *Early American Songbook*. Englewood Cliffs, NJ: Prentice Hall, 1974. 153pp. Arr. for piano.

This book provides 63 songs from the colonial and Revolutionary War periods, with very brief notes.

30 / SOCIAL STUDIES

 Further Reading

97. Smith, Carleton Sprague. "Broadsides and Their Music in Colonial America," In *Music in Colonial Massachusetts, 1630-1820.* 2 vols. Boston: The Colonial Society of Massachusetts, 1980. 157–368.

    Broadsides are single sheets of paper that were often used in Colonial America to carry the texts of songs. Basically narrative, these songs told of military events, supernatural happenings, tales of woe, sudden deaths or accidents, unusual adventures, and topical events. Flourishing between the eighteenth century and the Civil War, they were often sold by peddlers. Facsimile reproductions, background information, text, and melodies for more than 50 songs are provided.

American Revolution

(*See also* American History: General)

Monday, August 14, 1769
Dined with 350 Sons of Liberty at Robinsons, the Sign of Liberty Tree in Dorchester... After Dinner was over and the Toasts drank... we had also the Liberty Song—that by the Farmer... and the whole Company joined in the Chorus.
    This is cultivating the Sensations of Freedom.
■ John Adams, *Diary*

I have great faith in the influence of songs; and shall continue, while fulfilling the duties of my appointment [as chaplain], to write one now and then, and to encourage the taste for them which I find in the camp. One good song is worth a dozen addresses and proclamations.
■ Joel Barlow, Connecticut poet, 1777

 Article

98. *Seidman, Laurence I. "Teaching About the American Revolution Through Its Folk Songs," *Social Education* 37, no. 7 (November, 1973): 653–61. Arr. for guitar. Grades 4+.

    The author notes the importance of folksongs for teaching and understanding the Revolutionary War period. The text, melody, and brief background notes are provided for the following songs: "The Liberty Song"; "The Parody to the Liberty Song"; "To the Ladies"; "Castle Island Song"; "Rich Old Lady"; "The British Grenadiers"; "Trip to Cambridge"; "Sir Peter Parker"; "Battle of Saratoga"; "Johnny Has Gone for a Soldier"; "Ballad of André"; and "Cornwallis's Country Dance." A bibliography and discography are provided.

Books

99. Silber, Irwin. *Songs of Independence*. Harrisburg, PA: Stackpole Books, 1973. 178pp. Arr. for guitar.
    This extensive collection of 97 songs and ballads is arranged chronologically and includes an historical background. A bibliography and discography are provided.

100. *Silverman, Jerry. *Songs and Stories from the American Revolution*. Brookfield, CT: Millbrook Press, 1994. 72pp. [P] Grades 5+.
    This is a collection of 11 songs from the American Revolution with well-written explanations of each song's history and meaning. Songs provided are: "The Drum"; "The Wars of America"; "The Sergeant"; "Yankee Doodle"; "Ballad of Bunker Hill"; "Riflemen of Bennington"; "Battle of Saratoga"; "Swamp Fox"; "Surrender of Cornwallis"; and "In the Days of Seventy-Six." A bibliography is included.

 Pamphlets

101. *Scott, John Anthony, and Laurence I. Seidman. "Songs of the American Revolution, 1776–1777," *Folksong in the Classroom* 3, no. 1 (fall 1982): 6–26. [Reprinted vol. 15, no. 1-3, 1994-1995] (P.O. Box 925, Sturbridge, MA 01566) Arr. for guitar. Grades 5+. [ED 391704]
    A consistently excellent source of songs and information dedicated to enriching the study of social studies, literature, and the humanities (K-12) through the use of folksong, this issue offers 15 songs from the American Revolution period with background notes, as well as suggested activities and literature tie-ins. Songs include: "Young Ladies in Town"; "Liberty Song and a Parody, 1768"; "Castle Island Song"; "The Rich Old Lady"; "Fish and Tea"; "A Junto Song"; "Irishman's Epistle"; "The Deserter"; "British Grenadiers"; "Trip to Cambridge"; "Sir Peter Parker"; "Dying Redcoat"; and "Battle of Trenton."

102. *———. "Songs of the American Revolution, 1777-1783," *Folksong in the Classroom* 3, no. 2 (spring 1983): 30–54. [Reprinted vol. 15, no. 1-3, 1994–1995] (P.O. Box 925, Sturbridge, MA 01566) Arr. for guitar. Grades 5+. [ED 391704]
    A continuation of the previous issue, this issue contains the following songs: "Battle of Saratoga"; "The Fate of John Burgoyne"; "How Stands the Glass Around?"; "The Battle of the Kegs"; "Johnny Has Gone for a Soldier"; "High Germany"; "Paul Jones"; "The Ballad of Major André"; "A New Song, Written by a Soldier"; "The Battle of King's Mountain"; and "Cornwallis's Surrender and Country Dance." A bibliography and discography are included.

32 / SOCIAL STUDIES

 Recordings

103. **American Revolution Through Its Songs and Ballads.* Performed and narrated by Bill Bonyun and J. Anthony Scott. Heirloom Records HL-502. (Route 2, Wiscasset, ME 04518) LP. Grades 3+.
   This recording features skillful interweaving of songs and narrative and comes with a pamphlet containing lyrics and background information. Titles include: "The Liberty Song"; "Revolutionary Tea"; "Fish and Tea"; "The Irishman's Epistle"; "The Dying Redcoat"; "To the Ladies"; "Nathan Hale"; "Battle of Trenton"; "Riflemen of Bennington"; "How Stands the Glass Around?"; "The Battle of the Kegs"; "Shule Aroon"; "Ballad of Paul Jones"; "Ballad of Major André"; and "The Country Dance."

104. **Colonial and Revolution Songs.* Performed by Keith McNeil and Rusty McNeil. WEM Records. (16230 VanBuren Boulevard, Riverside, CA 92504) audiocassette and compact disc. Grades 4+.
   This recording provides 40 songs with narration and an accompanying songbook. Titles in the Revolutionary War section include: "British Grenadiers"; "Free America"; "Castle Island Song"; "Rich Lady over the Sea"; "Yankee Doodle"; "Battle of the Kegs"; "Chester"; "Johnny Has Gone for a Soldier"; "The World Turned Upside Down"; and "Hail Columbia."

105. **Voices of American History: Vol. I, Pre-Colonial Through the Revolutionary War.* By Steven Traugh. Cypress, CA: Creative Teaching Press, 1994. audiocassette. Grades 4+.
   This tape comes with a 38-page booklet containing narratives, lyrics, activities, and performance tips. Songs and narratives are on one side of the tape with music only on the second side for accompanying class performances. Songs relating to the Revolution are: "British Grenadiers"; "Revolutionary Tea"; "Free America"; "Revolutionary War Medley" ("Yankee Doodle," "Song of the Minutemen," "Yankee Privateer," "Johnny Has Gone for a Soldier," "Old Soldiers of the King," "World Turned Upside Down"); and "Hail Columbia."

 Further Sources of Songs

106. Rabson, Carolyn. *Songbook of the American Revolution.* Peaks Island, ME: Neo Press, 1974. 112pp. [P]
   A number of lesser-known Revolutionary War songs are presented here and include brief introductions and notes. A bibliography is provided.

107. Vinson, Lee. *Early American Songbook*. Englewood Cliffs, NJ: Prentice Hall, 1974. 153pp. Arr. for piano.

This book provides 63 songs, ballads, and brief notes from the colonial and Revolutionary War periods.

 Further Reading

108. Bowman, Kent H. *A Century of Liberty and War Songs, 1765–1865*. New York: Greenwood, 1985. 172pp.

Analysis and description of Revolutionary War songs are provided in this scholarly treatise, including history, uses, and meanings. There is no music and few texts.

109. Coffin, Tristram Potter. *Uncertain Glory: Folklore and the American Revolution*. Reprint. Detroit, MI: Gale Research, 1971. 270pp.

Several chapters on folksongs and the American Revolution are included in this collection of essays by a leading folklorist.

110. Lemay, J. A. Leo. "The American Origins of 'Yankee Doodle,'" *William and Mary Quarterly*, 3d series, 33 (July 1976): 435–64.

This is the best study to date on one of America's best-known songs. Readers may be surprised to learn the song did not originate in Connecticut and predates both the French and Indian War and the American Revolution.

111. Schrader, Arthur. "Songs to Cultivate the Sensations of Freedom," *Music in Colonial Massachusetts, 1630–1820*. vol. I. Boston: The Colonial Society of Massachusetts, 1980. 105–56.

Schrader, a leading authority on early American song, provides a thorough treatment of Revolutionary War broadsides. Facsimile copies are provided for 17 songs with melodies.

112. Scott, John Anthony. "Ballads and Broadsides of the Revolution," *Sing Out!* (April/May, 1966):18–23. Arr. for guitar. [P] Grades 5+.

This article offers an analysis of the political and ideological uses of songs during the Revolution and includes such songs as "Paul Jones' Victory," "A Junto Song," and "The Deserter."

113. *Wilson, Ruth Mack, with the assistance of Kate Van Winkle Keller. *Connecticut's Music in the Revolutionary Era*. Connecticut Bicentennial Series no. XXXI. Hartford, CT: The American Revolution Bicentennial Commission of Connecticut, 1979. 142pp. [P]

Wilson provides an excellent examination of military, sacred, and recreational music in eighteenth-century Connecticut.

The Federal Period (1786–1801)

(*See also* American History: General)

 Pamphlets

114. *Scott, John Anthony, and Laurence I. Seidman. "The Federal Period, 1786–1801," *Folksong in the Classroom* VIII, no. 1 (fall 1987): 36. (P.O. Box 925, Sturbridge, MA 01566) Arr. for guitar. Grades 5+. [ED 308107]
      This article provides 13 songs from the Federal period and includes historical information and follow-up activities. Titles provided are: "God Save Great Washington"; "Raising of the New Roof"; "A Yankee Federal Song"; "Rights of Women"; "The Desponding Negro"; "Oh Dear, What Can the Matter Be?"; "XYZ"; "Green Grow the Rushes O"; "Hail Columbia"; "Patriotic Exultation on Lyon's Release"; "Federalist and Republican Parodies"; "Jefferson and Liberty"; and "Two Sisters."

115. *———. "The U.S. Constitution Through Its Songs and Ballads," *Folksong in the Classroom* VII, no. 1 (fall 1986): 3–43. (P.O. Box 925, Sturbridge, MA 01566) Arr. for guitar. Grades 5+. [ED 344784]
      The authors, both with extensive teaching backgrounds, present an excellent guide for examining the history and ideas of the Constitution and the Bill of Rights through songs. Introductory material and follow-up activities are included. Titles include: "Fish and Tea"; "New Song, Written By a Soldier"; "To the West"; "My Fancy Flies Free"; "The Quaker's Courtship"; "Take This Hammer"; "Bread and Roses"; "Wanderin'"; "Going down the Road"; "Teacher's Lament"; and "Taxation Tyranny." A topical index is provided of songs from previous issues that can be used to illuminate the Constitution and Bill of Rights.

 Further Source of Songs

116. Silber, Irwin. *Songs of Independence*. Harrisburg, PA: Stackpole Books, 1973. 178pp. Arr. for guitar.
      Although primarily dealing with Revolutionary period songs and ballads, this work also includes a chapter on songs of the new nation and the War of 1812. Songs include: "A Yankee Federal Song"; "The Hobbies"; "Hail Columbia"; "Gunpowder Tea"; "The *Constitution* and the *Guerrière*"; "Come All You Bold Canadians"; "The *Shannon* and the *Chesapeake*"; "Perry's Victory"; "James Bird"; "Ye Parliament of England"; "The Patriotic Diggers"; "The Star-Spangled Banner"; "The Noble Lads of Canada"; "The Battle of New Orleans"; and "Old England Forty Years Ago." A bibliography and discography are provided.

War of 1812

(*See also* American History: General)

Pamphlet

117. *Scott, John Anthony, and Laurence I. Seidman. "Jefferson, Madison and War of 1812, (1801–1814)," *Folksong in the Classroom* VIII, no. 2 (winter 1988): 40–71. (P.O. Box 925, Sturbridge, MA 01566) Arr. for guitar. Grades 5+. [ED 308107]
    This consistently useful resource provides an historical synopsis of the War of 1812 along with notes for the following songs: "Acquisition of Louisiana"; "On the Murder of Hamilton"; "Discoveries of Captain Lewis"; "The Embargo"; "John John"; "Napoleon Bonaparte"; "Bonny Bunch of Roses O"; "General Brock"; "Defense of Fort McHenry" ("Star-Spangled Banner"); "*Constitution* and the *Guerrière*"; "Johnny Bull, My Jo, John"; "*Shannon* and the *Chesapeake*"; "James Bird"; and "Hunters of Kentucky." Suggestions for classroom follow-up activities are also provided.

Recordings

118. *Ballads of the War of 1812, 1791–1836.* Performed by Wallace House. Smithsonian/Folkways 05002, Washington, DC. 2 audiocassette set.
    This recording provides descriptive notes and lyrics. Titles include: "Eighth Day of November"; "Hail Columbia"; "Song of the Vermonters"; "Jefferson and Liberty"; "Johnny Has Gone for a Soldier"; "Benny Havens, O"; "Hey Betty Martin"; "Come All Bold Canadians"; "*Constitution* and *Guerrière*"; "Chare the Can Cheerily"; "Hornet and the Peacock"; "*Shannon* and the *Chesapeake*"; "Perry's Victory on Lake Erie"; "James Bird"; "Battle of Stonington"; "Ye Parliament of England"; "Star-Spangled Banner"; "Patriotic Diggers"; "Hunters of Kentucky"; "Yankee Volunteer"; "Old England Forty Years Ago"; "Hail Africa Band"; "Andrew Jackson"; "Harrison Song"; and "Aroostook War."

119. *Colonial and Revolution Songs.* Performed by Keith McNeil and Rusty McNeil. WEM Records. (16230 Van Buren Boulevard, Riverside, CA 92504) audiocassette and compact disc, 120 min. Accompanying songbook. Grades 3+.
    Part IV of a two-set collection covers the War of 1812. Titles include: "The Eighth of January"; "Sinclair's Defeat"; "Parliament of England"; "Noble Lads of Canada"; "The *Constitution* and the *Guerrière*"; "To Anacreon in Heaven"; "Patriotic Diggers"; and "Hunters of Kentucky."

36 / SOCIAL STUDIES

 Further Source of Songs

120. Silber, Irwin. *Songs of Independence*. Harrisburg, PA: Stackpole Books, 1973. 178pp. Arr. for guitar.
    Although primarily focusing on Revolutionary period songs and ballads, this work also includes a chapter on songs of the new nation and the War of 1812. Songs, with historical context, include: "A Yankee Federal Song"; "The Hobbies"; "Hail Columbia"; "Gunpowder Tea"; "*Constitution* and the *Guerrière*"; "Come All You Bold Canadians"; "*Shannon* and the *Chesapeake*"; "Perry's Victory"; "James Bird"; "Ye Parliament of England"; "The Patriotic Diggers"; "The Star-Spangled Banner"; "The Noble Lads of Canada"; "The Battle of New Orleans"; and "Old England Forty Years Ago." Includes a bibliography and a discography.

 Further Reading

121. Bowman, Kent H. *A Century of Liberty and War Songs, 1765-1865*. New York: Greenwood, 1985. 172pp.
    This work offers a scholarly analysis and description of war songs (including War of 1812) as well as the history, uses, and meanings behind those songs. It does not provide music, and few texts are included.

Industrial Revolution

(*See* Occupations: Miners, Mill Workers; Transportation: Canal, Trains. *See also* American History: General)

Westward Expansion

(*See also* American History: General, Gold Rush; Native Americans; Occupations: Cowboy; Regions: Southwest, West; Transportation: Trains)

 Article

122. *Kracht, James B. "Perceptions of the Great Plains in Nineteenth Century Folk Song: Teaching About Place," *Journal of Geography* 88, no. 6 (November/December 1989): 206–12. Grades 4+.
    Kracht explains how geography's impact on peoples' lives is sometimes reflected in folksong. Teacher preparation material is provided, along with a sample lesson plan with music and lyrics for

four songs: "Home on the Range"; "Lane County Bachelor" ("Starving to Death on My Government Claim"); "Dakota (Nebraska) Land"; and "The Kansas Fool." Includes a bibliography.

Pamphlet

123. *Scott, John A., and Laurence Seidman. "The Westward Movement: The Pioneers, the Indians and the Frontier, 1750–1810," *Folksong in the Classroom* V, no. 1 (autumn 1984): 8-22. (P.O. Box 925, Sturbridge, MA 01566) Arr. for guitar. Grades 5+.

This pamphlet describes how songs chronicle the story of one of the most important themes in American history, the clearing and settling of the American wilderness. Demonstrating this idea, the authors—themselves teachers with extensive experience in using songs in the classroom—give good introductory and background notes for the following songs: "Cumberland Gap"; "Battle of Point Pleasant"; "Logan's Complaint"; "St. Clair's Defeat"; "Wagoner's Lad"; "Old Joe Clark"; "Six Little Mice"; "Alphabet Song"; "Pleasant Ohio"; and "Three Jolly Hunters." Suggestions for follow-up activities are also provided.

Recordings

124. *Frontier Ballads.* Performed by Pete Seeger. Smithsonian/Folkways 02175, Washington, DC. audiocassette and compact disc.

Descriptive notes and lyrics are provided with this recording of popular titles such as: "Fare You Well, Polly"; "No Irish Need Apply"; "Johnny Gray"; "Greer County Bachelor"; "Cowboy Yodel"; "Trail to Mexico"; "Joe Bowers"; "Wake Up, Jacob"; "Cumberland Gap"; "Erie Canal"; "Blow the Man Down"; "Ox Driver's Song"; "Texan Boys"; "Sioux Indians"; "Ground Hog"; "Blue Mountain Lake"; "Paddy Works on the Railway"; "Young Man Who Wouldn't Hoe Corn"; "Joe Clark"; "My Sweetheart in the Mines"; "Holler"; "Arkansas Traveler"; "When I Was Single"; "Wondrous Love"; "Play Party"; "Whiskey, Rye, Whiskey"; and "Wayfaring Stranger."

125. *Moving West.* Performed by Keith McNeil and Rusty McNeil. WEM Records. (16230 Van Buren Boulevard, Riverside, CA 92504) audiocassette and compact disc. Grades 5+.

This recording combines narration and songs and covers such topics as: abolition; the Texan-Mexican War; the California gold rush; and immigration from China, Ireland, and Germany. Titles include: "Old Rosin the Beau"; "To the West"; "The Erie Canal"; "Wisconsin Emigrant"; "Shanty-Man's Life"; "Jam on Gerry's Rocks"; "Shenandoah"; "Darling Nellie Gray"; "Steal Away";

"Abolitionist Hymn"; "Follow the Drinking Gourd"; "Cielito Lindo"; "El Capotin"; "Texas Rangers"; "Texas War Cry"; "Will You Come to the Bower"; "Zachary Taylor"; "Mormon Battalion Song"; "Buck Him and Gag Him"; "The Life I Left Behind Me"; "Las Mañanitas"; "Old Dan Tucker"; "Camptown Races"; "Hard Times Come Again No More"; "Oh, California"; "Crossing the Plains"; "Days of Forty-Nine"; "Square Dance"; "California Ball"; "Sweet Betsy from Pike"; "California As It Is"; "Heathen Chinese"; "John Chinaman"; "John Chinaman's Appeal"; "Famine Song"; "No Irish Need Apply"; "Who Threw the Overalls in Mrs. Murphy's Chowder?"; "Lather 'n' Shave Em"; "The Night That Paddy Murphy Died"; "The Bold Fenian Men"; "Die Gedanken Sind Frei"; "O Tannenbaum"; and "Du, Du, Liegst Mir Im Herzen."

126. *Touch the Past: A Musical Diary of a Pioneer Family's Journey West. Performed by Esther Kreek, 1984. (St. Joseph Museum, 11th & Charles St., St. Joseph, MO 64501) audiocassette. Grades 3+.

Twenty-two traditional songs are presented on the tape that were popular along the wagon trails in the 1850s and 1860s. A booklet is included that presents music and lyrics, a diary keyed to the music, and a bibliography. The following titles are provided: "Miss McCleod's Reel/Leather Breeches"; "Flop-Eared Mule"; "Amazing Grace"; "What Was Your Name in the States?"; "Girl I Left Behind Me"; "Swing Low, Sweet Chariot"; "Paper of Pins"; "Buckeye Jim"; "Buffalo Gals"; "Oh Susannah"; "Arkansas Traveler"; "St. Anne's Reel/Soldier's Joy"; "All Through the Night"; "Billy Boy"; "Old Brass Wagon"; "Flow Gently, Sweet Afton"; "Blue-Tail Fly"; "Dakotah Indian Melody"; "Haste to the Wedding"; and "Wondrous Love."

127. *Voices of American History: Vol. III, The Westward Expansion of the United States. By Steven Traugh. Cypress, CA: Creative Teachers Press, 1994. audiocassette. Grades 4–6.

This tape of songs with narrative comes with a 40-page booklet containing text, lyrics, activities, and performance tips. Songs and narratives are on the first tape. The second tape has music only for accompanying class performance. Titles presented are: "Cumberland Gap"; "Lovely Ohio"; "To the West"; "Shenandoah"; "Texas and Mexican War Medley" ("Cielito Lindo," "Remember the Alamo"); "Sweet Betsy from Pike"; "California Gold Rush Medley" ("Oh, California," "A Chinese-American Doodle"); "Starving to Death on a Government Claim"; "Jam on Jerry's Rock"; "Drill Ye Tarriers, Drill"; "Little Bighorn"; "Old Chisholm Trail"; and "America the Beautiful."

128. *The Winning of the West*. Performed by Tom Glazer. 4 records. CMS 670. vol. 3 of The Musical Heritage of America collection. 1974. LP. Grades 4+.
   Descriptive notes are provided in this recording along with these titles: "Great Granddad"; "Sherman Cyclone"; "Common Bill"; "Lane County Bachelor"; "Housewife's Lament"; "Home on the Range"; "Old Settler's Song"; "I Ride an Old Paint"; "Git Along Little Dogies"; "Old Chisholm Trail"; "Sioux Indians"; "Streets of Laredo"; "Custer's Last Charge"; "Frankie and Johnny"; "Roving Gambler"; "Jesse James"; "Duncan and Brady"; "Sam Bass"; "In the Days of '49"; "Sacramento"; "Clementine"; "Pike County Miner"; "Sweet Betsy from Pike"; "He's the Man for Me"; "Pat Works on the Railway"; "Casey Jones"; "She'll Be Coming Round the Mountain"; "Midnight Special"; "John Henry"; "Hallelujah I'm a Bum"; "Jam on Gerry's Rocks"; "On the Banks of the Little Eau Pleine"; "Frozen Logger"; "River in the Pines"; "Flat River Girl"; "I Wish I Was Single Again"; "Raise a Ruckus"; "Oh, Susannah"; "Old Dan Tucker"; "Blue-Tail Fly"; "Green Grow the Lilacs"; "Have You Struck Ile"; "Little Old Sod Shanty"; "Elanoy"; "Dakota Land"; and "Buffalo Skinners."

 Further Sources of Songs

129. Lingenfelter, Richard E., Richard A. Dwyer, and David Cohen. *Songs of the American West*. Los Angeles: University of California Press, 1968. 595pp.
   Songs of traveling overland and 'round the Horn, the railroad, mining, Mormons, Indians, cowboys, and farming the prairie can be found here. Unfortunately there is no background information on individual songs.

130. Lomax, Alan. *Folk Songs of North America*. New York: Doubleday, 1960. 623pp. Arr. for piano and guitar. [P]
   This is a great collection by one of America's foremost authorities on folksong. The chapter on pioneers and the section on the West are recommended.

131. *Silber, Irwin, and Earl Robinson. *Songs of the Great American West*. 1967. Reprint, New York: Dover Publications, 1995. 334pp.
   Notes on the social and historical significance of 89 songs are found in this book. Topics include cowboys, the gold rush, Mexican American conflict, farmers, and outlaws. A bibliography, discography, and subject index are provided.

132. Silverman, Jerry. *Songs of the Western Frontier*. Pacific, MO: Mel Bay, 1992. 111pp. Arr. for piano and guitar. [P]
   A prolific compiler of song anthologies, Silverman offers a collection of songs that chronicle America's western history. Songs of cowboys, outlaws, and overland travel are all represented.

The Gold Rush

(See also **American History: General, Western Expansion; Regions: Southwest, West; Occupations: Miners; States: California)**

 Book

133. *Dwyer, Richard, and Richard Lingenfelter. *Songs of the Gold Rush.* Los Angeles: University of California Press, 1964. 199pp. Arr. for guitar. [P]
    Eighty-eight songs and commentary on the often tragic story of the California gold rush comprise this collection.

 Pamphlet

134. *Scott, John A., and Laurence I. Seidman. "Songs of the California Gold Rush," *Folksong in the Classroom* 3, no. 3 (spring 1983): 70–81. (P.O. Box 925, Sturbridge, MA 01566) Arr. for guitar. Grades 5+.
    Developed by two teachers with extensive experience using folksongs in the classroom, each issue of this excellent resource focuses on a different topic covered in the social studies, literature, or humanities classroom. This issue deals with the California gold rush. Introductory and background notes provide historical and social context for the following songs: "Fools of '49"; "Santy Anno"; "Sweet Betsy from Pike"; "The Lousy Miner"; "Miners' Meeting"; "Dying Californian"; "Days of '49"; and "Far California." The unit ends with suggested follow-up activities for the classroom. A bibliography and discography are provided.

 Recording

135. *Days of '49: Songs of the Gold Rush.* Performed by Logan English. Smithsonian/Folkways 05255, Washington, DC, 1957. audiocassette and compact disc.
    Descriptive notes and lyrics are provided in this recording, which includes these titles: "Sacramento"; "A Ripping Trip"; "Sweet Betsy from Pike"; "Crossing the Plains"; "Prospecting Dream"; "Life in California"; "Days of '49"; "He's the Man for Me"; "Clementine"; "The Gambler"; "Joe Bowers"; "The California State Company"; "California Bloomer"; and "Sacramento Gals."

Immigration

(*See also* World Cultures)

IRISH IMMIGRATION

 Pamphlet

136. Scott, John Anthony. "Irish Immigration Through Its Songs and Ballads," *Folksong in the Classroom* XII, no. 2 (winter 1992): 3–32. (P.O. Box 925, Sturbridge, MA 01566) Arr. for guitar. [P] Grades 5+.
    This issue of a newsletter for social studies, language arts, and humanities teachers presents a script written and performed by American history classes at Fieldston School in New York in 1963. It is an example of how students can more actively participate in their own learning. Songs include: "The Jackets Green"; "Caitilin Ni Uallachain"; "Brennan on the Moor"; "Roddy McCorley"; "Shtaradahdey"; "Mrs. McGrath"; "The Praties They Grow Small"; "The Farmer's Cursed Wife"; "Working on the Railway"; and "The Jug of Punch." A bibliography is provided.

 Recording

137. *Farewell to Eirinn*. Performed by Delores Keane and John Faulkner. Green Linnet #3003. (43 Beaver Brook Road, Danbury, CT 06810) audiocassette and compact disc. Grades 6+.
    Traditional Irish songs tell the history of Irish immigration in the songs performed in this recording. Titles include: "Farewell to Ireland"; "Paddy's Green Shamrock Shore"; "Edward Conners"; "The Kilnamiarty Emigrant"; "Reels" ("Staten Island," "Greenfields of America"); "Sleibh Gallion Braes"; "Cragie Hills"; "Farmer Michael Hayes"; "Reels" ("Maid of Mt. Kisco," "Farewell to Connaught," "Farewell to Ireland"); and "Greenfields of America."

FRENCH CANADIAN

 Recording

138. *Chanterelle: French in America*. Performed by Chanterelle. (Cevon Musique, P.O. Box 2235, Amherst, MA 01004) audiocassette and compact disc. Grades 5+.
    This recording features both traditional and contemporary songs. Titles include: "Les Flammes d'Enfer"; "Millworkers Medley"; "French in America"; "Leavin' Train"; "Tunes" ("Fireside Reel," "Two Step," "d'Armand," "Reel Béatrice"); "Lullaby/Berceuse"; "Dondaine

la Ridaine"; "Ma Mère Chantait"; "La Robe Barrée"; "Tunes" ("Brasstown," "Uncle Bob's Boogie"); and "Un Canadien Errant."

Slavery

(*See also* African American; American History: General, The Civil War)

 Article

139. *Lord, Donald C. "The Slave Song as a Historical Source," *Social Education* 35, no. 7 (November 1971): 763–69. Grades 5+.
 Lord highlights the value of slave music as an historical source of information and offers a lesson plan (with words only) to: "Follow the Drinking Gourd"; "Freedom Land, All My Trials"; "Oh My God, Them Taters"; "Good News, Member"; "The Blue-Tail Fly"; and "Oh, Freedom."

 Pamphlet

140. *Chilcoat, George. "Teaching About Slavery Through Folk Song," *Folksong in the Classroom* IV, no. 3 (May 1984): 62–81. (P.O. Box 925, Sturbridge, MA 01566) Grades 5+. [ED 273507]
 The author describes how he used songs to teach a unit on slavery and what the educational impact was. Song lyrics and melodies are provided for the following songs: "Pick a Bale of Cotton"; "Long Summer Day"; "Man Goin' Round"; "Sold Off to Georgy"; "Sometimes I Feel Like a Motherless Child"; "Michael, Row the Boat Ashore"; "Nobody Knows the Trouble I've Seen"; "Follow the Drinking Gourd"; "Go Down, Moses"; "All God's Children Got Shoes"; "Steal Away"; "I'm on My Way"; "Oh, Freedom"; and "Roll, Jordan, Roll." A bibliography is included.

 Recording

141. *Music and the Underground Railroad*. Performed by Kim Harris and Reggie Harris. Ascension Productions, 1988. (P.O. Box 18871, Philadelphia, PA 19119) audiocassette. Grades 3–5.
 Traditional and original songs are presented to tell the story of the underground railroad. Songs include such titles as: "This Little Light of Mine"; "No More Auction Block for Me"; "Let Us Break Bread Together on Our Knees"; "Ballad of the Underground Railroad"; "Follow the Drinking Gourd"; "Harriet Tubman/Steal Away"; "Go Down Moses"; "Trampin'"; "One More River to Cross"; "Ballad of Crispus Attucks"; and "Free At Last." A reproducible teacher's guide and poster are also included.

Further Sources of Songs

142. Allen, William Francis, Charles Pickard Ware, and Lucy McKim Garrison. *Slave Songs of the United States*. 1867. Reprint, New York: Dover Publications, 1995. 115pp.
    This is an important pioneer collection of Sea Island slave songs collected during the Civil War.

143. *Silverman, Jerry. *Slave Songs*. New York: Chelsea House, 1994. 80pp. Arr. for piano. [P] Grades 5+.
    This is a good collection of more than two dozen songs performed by Afro-American slaves, with an introduction and brief notes for each song.

 Further Reading

144. Courlander, Harold. *Negro Folk Music, U.S.A.* New York: Columbia University Press. 1963. Reprint, New York: Dover Publications, 1992. 324pp.
    See the chapter on slave songs for interesting background information. A bibliography and discography are provided.

145. Goines, Dr. Leonard. "'Walk Over!': Music in the Slave Narratives," *Sing Out!* 24, no. 6 (1976): 6–11. (P.O. Box 5253, Bethlehem, PA 18015)
    For this article Goines studied slave narratives for information on plantation dances and instrumental and vocal music. Music and lyrics are given for "Many Thousand Gone" and "Round the Corn, Sally."

146. Greenway, John. *American Folksongs of Protest*. 1953. Reprint, Philadelphia: University of Pennsylvania Press, 1960. 348pp.
    This book presents the history of protest song in America by dividing the chapters into songs of Afro-Americans, textile workers, miners, migrant workers, farmers, and others. Almost no music is provided. See the chapter titled "Negro Songs of Protest" for a good discussion on slave songs. A discography and bibliography are included.

147. *Jones, Arthur C. *Wade in the Water: The Wisdom of the Spirituals*. Maryknoll, NY: Orbis Books, 1993. 182pp.
    This work gives an excellent review of the literature and analysis of spirituals, including their development, meaning, and use from slave times to the present, particularly in reference to their psychological importance.

148. Levine, Laurence W. "Slave Songs and Slave Consciousness: An Exploration of Neglected Sources," in *Anonymous Americans: Explorations in 19th Century Social History*, edited by Tamara Harever, 89–130. Englewood, NJ: Prentice Hall, 1971.

>This is an excellent essay on the various ways songs served slaves, including providing a sense of community, a "safety-valve" for feelings of oppression and depression, and a medium for resistance.

The Civil War and Reconstruction

(*See also* American History: General, Slavery)

 Article

149. Anastasio, Joseph L. "The Reconstruction Era: The Night They Drove Old Dixie Down," *Teacher* (February 1981): 74–75. Grades 7+.

>This is a good lesson plan on a song that helps students understand the reconstruction era. An explanation of historical context is given, and lyrics are included, but no melody is provided.

 Books

150. Glass, Paul. *Singing Soldiers: A History of the Civil War in Song*. 1964. Reprint, New York: Da Capo Press, 1975. Arr. for piano and guitar. [P] (Originally titled *The Spirit of the Sixties*) 300pp.

>This is a collection of more than 100 songs, with music and introductory notes. A bibliography is provided.

151. *Silber, Irwin. *Songs of the Civil War*. 1960. Reprint, New York: Dover Publications, 1997. 400pp. Arr. for piano and guitar.

>Containing 125 of the most popular Union and Confederate songs of the Civil War—songs of victory and defeat, sorrow and laughter, and heroism and homesickness—this is one of the best and most complete collections on this subject. A detailed account of each song's history, notes on the composer, a description of the circumstances under which it was written, as well as comments on the historical and social context are provided. A bibliography is included.

152. Silverman, Jerry. *Ballads and Songs of the Civil War*. Pacific, MO: Mel Bay Publications, 1994. 272pp. Arr. for piano and guitar. [P] Accompanying recording. Grades 5+.

>This anthology includes songs that deal with battles, abolitionists, spirituals, Lincoln, soldiers, and humor.

Pamphlet

153. * Scott, John Anthony, and Laurence I. Seidman. "Songs of the Civil War," *Folksong in the Classroom* II, no. 1 (October-November 1981): 6–21. (P.O. Box 925, Sturbridge, MA 01566) Grades 5+. [ED 273505]
    This newsletter, dedicated to enriching the teaching of social studies, literature, and the humanities for K-12, examines the Civil War with recruiting songs, marching and battle songs, sea songs, freedom songs, and songs of women. An introduction and commentary present the following songs in historical context: "Walking on the Green Grass"; "Yankee Man O War"; "Lowlands of Holland"; "Bonnie Blue Flag" (northern and southern versions); "Many Thousand Gone"; "The First of Arkansas"; "Roll, Alabama, Roll"; and "Southern Girl's Reply." Also included is a bibliography of children's books on the Civil War as well as a discography.
    [For a script for a seventh-grade student performance based on this theme, see John Anthony Scott, "The Civil War Through Its Songs and Ballads," *Folksong in the Classroom* XII, no. 3, (spring 1992): 6–31. Bibliography and classroom activities included.]

 Recordings

154. *The Civil War*. Performed by Tom Glazer. CMS 660. vol. 2 of The Musical Heritage of America collection. 1973. LP and audiocassette. Grades 4+.
    This recording presents songs and narrated introductions on the Civil War. Descriptive notes and lyrics are included. Titles performed are: "I Am Sold and Going to Georgia"; "Run to Jesus"; "Johnny, Won't You Ramble"; "Follow the Drinking Gourd"; "Oh, Freedom"; "Bright Sparkles"; "Aura Lea"; "John Brown's Body"; "Battle Hymn of the Republic"; "Dixie"; "Maryland, My Maryland"; "Yellow Rose of Texas"; "Bonnie Blue Flag"; "Battle Cry of Freedom"; "Wait for the Wagon"; "Raw Recruit"; "We Are Coming, Father Abraham"; "Upidee Song"; "Lorena"; "Goober Peas"; "Army Bean"; "All Quiet Along the Potomac"; "Tenting on the Old Camp Ground"; "Just Before the Battle, Mother"; "Weeping, Sad and Lonely"; "Tramp, Tramp, Tramp"; "Vacant Chair"; "Treasury Rats"; "Year of Jubilo"; "Wake Nicodemus"; "Marching Through Georgia"; "When Johnny Comes Marching Home"; "*Cumberland's* Crew"; "Hold the Fort"; "In Charleston Jail"; "General Patterson"; "For Bales"; "Cumberland Gap"; "Unreconstructed Rebel"; "Wearing of the Grey"; "Conquered Banner"; and "President's Grave."

155. *Civil War Songs*. Performed by Keith McNeil and Rusty McNeil. WEM Records. (16230 Van Buren Boulevard, Riverside, CA 92504) audiocassette and compact disc, 180 min. Grades 5+.

Sixty songs are presented here with dialogue covering slavery, the beginning of the war, President Lincoln, and more. Titles include: "All Quiet Along the Potomac Tonight"; "Lincoln and Liberty"; "Maryland, My Maryland"; "Bonnie Blue Flag"; "Yellow Rose of Texas"; "Just Before the Battle, Mother"; "Battle Hymn of the Republic"; "Battle of Shiloh Hill"; "Battle Cry of Freedom"; "Goober Peas"; "Homespun Dress"; "No More Auction Block for Me"; "Oh, Freedom"; "John Brown's Body"; "*Cumberland* and the *Merrimac*"; "The *Alabama*"; "Tramp, Tramp, Tramp"; "When Johnnie Comes Marching Home"; "Last Fierce Charge"; "Lorena"; "Aura Lea"; "Marching Through Georgia"; and "Tenting on the Old Camp Ground." Accompanied by a songbook.

156. **The Civil War Through Its Songs and Ballads*. Song and narration by Frank Warner, Bill Bonyun, and others. Heirloom Records. (Route 2, Wiscasset, ME 04518) LP. Grades 5+.

This recording features 24 songs with narrations based on primary sources (mostly contemporary letters) as well as good notes on the background of the songs. Titles performed include: "In the Wilderness"; "Old Abe Lincoln"; "Dissolution Wagon"; "John Brown of Massachusetts"; "Union Volunteer"; "Song of the Mississippi Volunteer"; "Aileen Aroon"; "Southern Yankee Doodle"; "Shiloh Hill"; "New Ballad of Lord Lovell"; "O Johnny Bull, My Jo John"; "Homespun Dress"; "We Have the Army"; "Maryland, My Maryland"; "General Lee's Wooing"; "Auction Block"; "First of Arkansas"; "Riding a Raid"; "Vacant Chair"; "Life on the Vicksburg Bluff"; "Sherman's March to the Sea"; "Grant the Man"; "Roll, Alabama, Roll"; and "Old Unreconstructed." A teacher's guide is provided.

157. *Johnny Whistlerigger* and *Rebel in the Woods: Civil War Songs from the Western Border, vols. 1 and 2*. Performed by Cathy Barton, Dave Para, and Bob Dyer. Big Canoe Records, 1995. (513 High Street, Booneville, MO 65233. Also available from Folk Legacy Records, Inc., Sharon, CT 06031) audiocassette and compact disc, 57 min. Grades 5+.

Each recording contains 15 traditional songs and narrations about the Civil War as it was fought in Missouri. A 40-page teacher's guide with lyrics and historical background on each song is included.

Titles on volume I include: "Marmaduke's Hornpipe"; "Abolitionist Hymn"; "Marais des Cygne"; "Song of the Kansas Immigrants/Call to Kansas"; "The Invasion of Camp Jackson"; "General Sigel's Grand March"; "I Goes to Fight Mit Sigel"; "Johnny Whistlerigger"; "Lyon's Funeral March"; "Honest Pat Murphy"; "Price's Proclamation"; "Battle of Pea Ridge"; "Muddy Road to Moberly"; "The Nature of the Guerilla"; "Quantrill Slide"; "Guerilla Man"; "Prairie

Grove"; "Kate's Song"; "The Last Great Rebel Raid"; "Shelby's Mule"; and "Knot of Blue and Gray."

Titles featured on volume II are: "The Call of Quantrill"; "The War in Missouri in '61"; "Missouri, Bright Land of the West"; "Atchison's Buchaneers/Quindaro Hornpipe"; "The Death of General Lyon"; "Kelly's Irish Brigade"; "Rebel in the Woods"; "The Swamp Fox"; "Daniel Martin"; "Marching Quadrille/Nolan the Soldier"; "The Blackfoot Rangers"; "Anderson's Warning"; "Wakefield"; "Jesse James"; and "Gone to Kansas."

158. *Songs of the Civil War*. Performed by various artists. Sony Music Video Enterprises. videocassette, 60 min.

This is a spin-off to the award-winning series on the Civil War by Ken Burns. It includes still photos and spoken passages along with live performances of Civil War songs performed by folk, country, bluegrass, gospel, and pop artists.

159. *Treasury of Civil War Songs*. Performed by Tom Glazer. Songs Music, Scarborough, NY, 1993. compact disc.

Titles featured on this disc of Civil War songs include: "John Brown's Body"; "Battle Hymn of the Republic"; "Dixie"; "Maryland, My Maryland"; "Yellow Rose of Texas"; "Bonnie Blue Flag"; "Upidee"; "Goober Peas"; "All Quiet on the Potomac"; "Tenting on the Old Camp Ground"; "Battle Cry of Freedom"; "Wait for the Wagon"; "We Are Coming Father Abraham"; "Just Before the Battle, Mother"; "Tramp, Tramp, Tramp"; "Year of Jubilo"; "Wake, Nicodemus"; "Marching Through Georgia"; "When Johnny Comes Marching Home"; "General Patterson"; "Cumberland Gap"; "Somebody's Darling"; "Conquered Banner"; and "President's Grave."

♪ Further Reading

160. Bowman, Kent H. *A Century of Liberty and War Songs, 1765-1865*. New York: Greenwood, 1985. 172pp.

This is a well-researched book with analyses and descriptions of war songs including their history, uses, and meaning. This book does not contain lyrics or music.

161. Heaps, Willard A., and Porter W. Heaps. *The Singing Sixties: The Spirit of the Civil War Days Drawn from the Music of the Times*. Norman, OK: University of Oklahoma Press, 1960. 423pp.

This work offers a close look at the songs of the Civil War, giving their history and significance. Major categories include rallying songs, lives of the soldiers in camp, battles, the folks at home, Black soldiers, and the war and its aftermath. Few melodies are given. A bibliography is provided.

162. *Sawyers, June Skinner. "The Blues and the Grays: Songs of the Civil War," *Sing Out!* 36, no. 3 (November/December 1991): 2–9.
>This article provides an excellent synopsis of the role of song during the Civil War as well as a brief but useful introduction to the topic. A bibliography and discography are included.

163. Stutler, Boyd B. "John Brown's Body," *Civil War History* 4 (1958): 285–89.
>For those who want to know more about the origins of this famous song, this article provides a good history.

The Great Depression and World War II

(*See also* **American History: General**)

If you can sing a song that would make people forget their troubles . . . I'll give you a medal.
> ■ Herbert Hoover to Rudy Valle

 ## Article

164. "Brother, Can You Spare a Dime?" *School Library Media Activities Monthly* XI, no. 8 (April 1995): 15–17. Grades 5+.
>This article offers suggestions for creating an integrated unit on the Great Depression. A bibliography and discography are provided.

 ## Pamphlet

165. *Scott, John Anthony, and Laurence I. Seidman. "The Depression and New Deal Through Songs and Ballads," *Folksong in the Classroom* XIII no. 2 (winter 1993): 2–41. (P.O. Box 925, Sturbridge, MA 01566) Arr. for guitar. Grades 7+.
>This resource for teachers of social studies, literature, and the humanities contains a script with 13 songs that can be used to help students explore the 1930s. An introduction with the historical background of the period is provided, along with suggestions for follow-up activities. Titles include: "Wandering"; "Everything Is Higher"; "Mouse's Courting Song"; "Soup Song"; "Raggedy"; "Times Are Gettin' Hard"; "We Shall Not Be Moved"; "Which Side Are You On?"; "Goin' Down the Road"; "Roll on Columbia"; "Strange Fruit"; "Discrimination Blues"; and "We Shall Overcome." A bibliography and discography are provided.

🎵 Recordings

166. *Dust Bowl Ballads*. Performed by Woody Guthrie. Smithsonian/Folkways 05212, Washington, DC, 1964. audiocassette and compact disc.

    Descriptive notes and lyrics are provided here, along with these songs: "Talkin' Dust Bowl"; "Blowin' Down This Road"; "Do-Re-Mi"; "Dust Cain't Kill Me"; "Tom Joad, Parts 1 & 2"; "The Great Dust Storm"; "So Long (Dusty Old Dust)"; "Dust Bowl Refugee"; "Dust Pneumonia Blues"; "I Ain't Got No Home in This World Anymore"; and "Vigilante Man."

167. *The Original "Talking Union" with the Almanac Singers and Other Union Songs with Peter Seeger and Chorus*. Smithsonian/Folkways FH 05285, Washington, DC. audiocassette and compact disc.

    Songs have long been a feature of labor unrest. During the 1930s and '40s the Almanac Singers were the most prominent song activists in the country. This recording contains descriptive notes as well as lyrics. Titles include: "We Shall Not Be Moved"; "Roll the Union On"; "Casey Jones"; "Miner's Lifeguard"; "Solidarity Forever"; "Join the Union"; "All I Want"; "Union Train"; "Talking Union"; and "Which Side Are You On?"

168. *Songs from the Depression*. Performed by New Lost City Ramblers. Smithsonian/Folkway 05264, Washington, DC. audiocassette and compact disc.

    Descriptive notes and texts to songs are provided with this recording. While popular music tried to provide an escape from hard times, songs such as these capture the hardships many people endured during the 1930s. Titles performed include: "No Depression in Heaven"; "There'll Be No Distinction There"; "Breadline Blues"; "White House Blues"; "Franklin Roosevelt's Back Again"; "How Can a Poor Man Stand Such Times and Live?"; "Keep Moving"; "Taxes on the Farmer Feeds Them All"; "Serves Them Fine"; "NRA Blues"; "Death of the Blue Eagle"; "Join the C.I.O."; "Old Age Pension Check"; "Sales Tax on the Women"; "Wreck of the Tennessee Gravy Train"; "Loveless C.C.C."; "Boys, My Money's All Gone"; and "All I Got's Gone."

169. *Woody Guthrie*. Princeton, NJ: Films for the Humanities and Sciences, FFH 1754, 1988. Videocassette, 13 min.

    "This Land Is Your Land" is only one of the many great songs written by Woody Guthrie. This video explores Woody Guthrie's life and his songs about working people.

Further Sources of Songs

170. Fowke, Edith, and Joe Glazer. *Songs of Work and Protest.* 1960. Reprint, New York: Dover Publications, 1973. 209pp. Arr. for guitar. [P]
>This collection features the songs of workers, working conditions, and labor movements from the 1930s. Brief introductory remarks as well as a bibliography and discography are provided.

171. Lomax, Alan, with Woody Guthrie and Pete Seeger. *Hard Hitting Songs for Hard-Hit People.* New York: Oak Publications, 1967. 368pp. Arr. for guitar. [P]
>More than 150 songs—industrial ballads, protest songs, and more—that were written during the Great Depression are collected here, including brief notes on each song.

 ## Further Reading

172. Brown, Sheldon. "The Depression and World War II As Seen Through Country Music," *Social Education* (October 1985): 588–95.
>This article examines the ways country music described the conditions and experiences of ordinary people during the 1930s and World War II. The article offers texts only, often just one or two verses. A bibliography and discography are provided.

Post World War II

(*See also* **American History: General**)

 ## Further Source of Songs

173. Glazer, Tom. *Songs of Peace, Freedom and Protest.* New York: Fawcett, 1972. Arr. for guitar. [P]
>This book features 81 songs, mostly from the 1960s, documenting political and social unrest of the period.

 ## Further Reading

174. Cooper, B. Lee. *The Popular Music Handbook: A Resource Guide for Teachers, Librarians, and Media Specialists.* Littleton, CO: Libraries Unlimited, 1984. 415pp. Grades 7+.
>A useful guide to popular music as it relates to specific themes in modern American culture, this resource provides units for teaching such diverse topics as Black life in America; city problems;

civil rights and equal opportunity; communication styles; ecology; economics; education; the future; generation gaps; urban life; issues of adolescence; law, order, and justice; propaganda; militarism and patriotism; the music business; old age and death; oral history; religion; outcasts; social mobility; technology; and women's liberation. A selected bibliography of music-oriented print resources by academic subject, along with bibliographies of popular music, songbooks, and lyric anthologies; biographical studies of pop music figures, composers, and lyricists; and discographies on popular styles, music composers, and performers are also included.

175. ———. "Popular Songs, Military Conflicts, and Public Perceptions of the United States at War," *Social Education* 56, no. 3 (March 1992): 160–68.
Changing images of war—World War I and II, Vietnam, and the Gulf War—as seen through popular song imagery is the focus of this article. A title list of selected war-related recordings and a bibliography are also provided.

176. ———. *A Resource Guide to Themes in Contemporary American Song Lyrics, 1950–1985*. Westport, CT: Greenwood, 1986. 481pp.
More than 3,000 popular recorded song titles are listed here to support the study of 15 social and political themes. Preceding each list is a brief essay. Themes covered include: characters and personalities; communication media; death; education; marriage, family life, and divorce; military conflicts; occupations, materialism, and the workplace; personal relationships, love, and sexuality; political protest and social criticism; poverty and unemployment; race relations; religion; transportation systems; urban life; and youth culture. Each major theme is divided into related sub-themes, and following each chapter is a discography and bibliography.

Civil Rights Movement

(*See also* American History: General)

 Books

177. *Carawan, Guy, and Candie Carawan. *Sing for Freedom: The Story of the Civil Rights Movement Through Its Songs*. Bethlehem, PA: Sing Out! 1990. (Reprint of *Freedom Is a Constant Struggle* and *We Shall Overcome*. New York: Oak Publications) 312pp. Arr. for guitar. [P]
This book documents the Civil Rights movement through its songs. A compact disc version (#40032) is available from Smithsonian/Folkways, Washington, DC.

52 / SOCIAL STUDIES

178. Seeger, Pete, and Robert S. Reiser. *Everybody Says Freedom: The Civil Rights Movement in Words, Pictures and Song*. New York: W. W. Norton & Company, 1990. 266pp. [P]

    This work covers the Civil Rights movement from 1955 to 1968 with songs, background information, and extended quotes from participants. Included are many songs from Carawan's *Sing for Freedom* (see entry 177). This book contains a bibliography.

179. Silverman, Jerry. *Songs of Protest and Civil Rights*. New York: Chelsea House, c.1992. 80pp. [P] Grades 5+.

    This is a collection of songs from the Civil Rights movement containing brief descriptive notes on each song and an informative introduction.

 ## Recordings

180. *Sing for Freedom: The Story of the Civil Rights Movement Through Its Songs*. Smithsonian/Folkways 40032, Washington, DC, 1990. audiocassette and compact disc, 60 min.

    This is an archival recording of songs sung at civil rights protests and meetings and presents excerpts from speeches given by civil rights leaders. Titles include: "We Are Soldiers in the Army"; "Keep Your Hand on the Plow"; "This Little Light"; "You Better Leave Segregation Alone"; "Your Dog Loves My Dog"; "Ain't Gonna Let Nobody Turn Me Around"; "I Woke Up This Morning with My Mind on Freedom"; "Keep Your Eyes on the Prize"; "Oh Pritchett, Oh Kelly"; "Up Above My Head"; "Brown Baby"; "Which Side Are You On?"; "I'm Gonna Sit at the Welcome Table"; "Mass Meeting and Prayer"; "Guide My Feet"; "I'm on My Way"; "Rev. Ralph Abernathy"; "Yes, We Want Our Freedom"; "Rev. Martin Luther King, Jr."; "Ninety-Nine and a Half Won't Do"; "Get on Board"; "No Danger in the Water"; "Medgar Evans Speaking"; "Keep Your Eyes on the Prize"; and "We Shall Overcome."

181. *Voices of the Civil Rights Movement: Black American Freedom Songs, 1960–1966*. Smithsonian Institution, Washington, DC, 1980. 3-volume set. audiocassette and compact disc.

    This is a collection of songs from the Civil Rights movement performed by such groups and individuals as the SNCC Freedom Singers, Fannie Lou Hamer, and Willis Peacock. The songs were recorded at public meetings between 1960 and 1966. Program notes and a discography come with the set.

182. *We Shall Overcome*. California News Reel, 1989. videocassette, 58 min.

    This is a PBS special that traces the origins and development of this traditional song from an old slave spiritual to its more recent use by labor and civil rights activists. Historical footage and personal recollections are included. Performances by Pete Seeger; Joan Baez; Taj Mahal; Peter, Paul and Mary; and the Freedom Singers are featured.

183. *We Shall Overcome: Songs of the Freedom Riders and the Sit-Ins.* Smithsonian/Folkways 05591, Washington, DC, 1961. audiocassette and compact disc.

Descriptive notes and lyrics are included in this recording featuring titles such as: "This Little Light of Mine"; "There's a Meeting Here Tonight"; "Rock My Soul"; "Hold On"; "Let Us Break Bread Together"; "We Are Soldiers in the Army"; "We Shall Not Be Moved"; "Your Dog"; "Michael Row the Boat Ashore"; "I'm So Glad"; and "Oh Freedom."

 For Further Reading

184. Sanger, Kerran L. *"When the Spirit Says Sing!" The Role of Freedom Songs in the Civil Rights Movement.* New York: Garland, 1995. 232pp.

This work discusses the importance of songs in the Civil Rights movement. A bibliography is provided.

Vietnam War

(*See also* **American History: General**)

 Article

185. Chilcoat, George W. "The Images of Vietnam: A Popular Music Approach," *Social Education* (October 1987): 601–3. Grades 7+.

Chilcoat discusses songs from the Vietnam War era according to the following themes: attitude towards war/Vietnam War, battle/soldiers, the draft, peace, attitudes toward society and government, and domestic events related to the war. One classroom activity is described and a bibliography is included.

Geography
(*See also* **Regions, States, Transportation, World Cultures**)

Land Forms

186. *Mulligan, Mary Ann. *Integrating Music with Other Studies.* New York: Center for Applied Research in Education, 1975. (521 Fifth Avenue, New York, NY 10017) 64pp. [P] Grades 1–4.

This book is a wonderful source of creative ideas for relating music to other subjects. The section titled "Exploring Concepts Related to Our Physical Environment" provides examples of how music can help children understand the idea of "desert," "plain," "mountain," "valley," "jungle," "rain forest," "coast," and "peninsula."

Government

Constitution and Bill of Rights

 Pamphlets

187. *Scott, John Anthony, and Laurence I. Seidman. "The Federal Period, 1786–1801," *Folksong in the Classroom* VIII, no. 1 (fall 1987): 1–36. (P.O. Box 925, Sturbridge, MA 01566) Arr. for guitar. Grades 7+. [ED 308107]
   Thirteen songs are presented here dealing with the federal period, plus introductory material and follow-up activities. Titles include: "God Save Great Washington"; "Raising of the New Roof"; "A Yankee Federal Song"; "Rights of Women"; "The Desponding Negro"; "Oh Dear, What Can the Matter Be?"; "XYZ"; "Green Grow the Rushes O"; "Hail Columbia"; "Patriotic Exultation on Lyon's Release"; "Federalist and Republican Parodies"; "Jefferson and Liberty"; and "Two Sisters."

188. *———. "The U.S. Constitution Through Its Songs and Ballads," *Folksong in the Classroom* VII, no. 1 (fall 1986): 1–40. (P.O. Box 925, Sturbridge, MA 01566). Arr. for guitar. Grades 5+. [ED 344784]
   Songs can help students understand abstract ideas. Developed by two teachers with extensive experience in using songs to explore history and the humanities, this excellent resource examines the history and ideas of the Constitution and the Bill of Rights through songs, with background information and follow-up activities. Titles include: "Fish and Tea;" "New Song, Written by a Soldier"; "To the West"; "My Fancy Flies Free"; "The Quaker's Courtship"; "Take This Hammer"; "Bread and Roses"; "Wanderin'"; "Going Down the Road"; "Teacher's Lament"; and "Taxation Tyranny." Also included is an index of songs that can be used to illuminate the Constitution and Bill of Rights, organized by topic—abuse of power, vision of freedom in the early republic and frontier, the protest and vision of the slaves, labor and the First Amendment, and the songs of women.

Elections

 Book

189. *Silber, Irwin. *Songs America Voted By*. Harrisburg, PA: Stackpole Books, 1971. 319pp. Arr. for guitar. [P]
    Silber has put together 200 songs ranging in historical context from 1768 to the campaign of Ronald Reagan. Each song is accompanied by good social and historical notes.

 Recording

190. *Election Songs of the United States*. Performed by Oscar Brand. Smithsonian/Folkways 05280, Washington, DC, 1960.
    For much of our history songs have been an important feature of political campaigns. While often simplistic, they highlight a candidate's (and era's) character and campaign theme(s). Brand, a well-known collector and singer of historical folksongs, has put together a compilation of these songs. A study guide and song lyric sheet are also included. Titles presented are: "Fair and Free Elections" (1800); "Jefferson and Liberty" (1800); "The Hunters of Kentucky" (1828); "Tyler and Tippicanoe" (1840); "Van Buren"; "Clay and Frelinghuysen" (1844); "Come Raise the Banner" (1844); "Freemont Train" (1856); "Little Mac Shall Be Restored" (1864); "Hurrah for Grant!" (1868); "Victoria's Banner" (1872); "The Boys in Blue" (1876); "For Victory Again" (1884); "His Grandfather's Hat" (1888); "When Grover's Term Comes to an End" (1888); "Shout McKinley" (1896); "Then and Now" (1900); "Roosevelt the Cry" (1904); "Al Smith" (1928); "If He's Good Enough for Lindy" (1928); "Cactus Jack and Franklin D." (1932); "We Want Wilkie" (1940); "I've Got a Ballot" (1948); and "The Presidents."

Holidays

 Books

191. Beggs-Cass, Barbara. *A Musical Calendar of Festivals: Folk Songs of Feast-Days and Holidays from Around the World*. London: Ward Lock Educational, 1983. 112pp. Arr. for guitar.
    This is a collection of almost 80 songs celebrating holidays and festivals from around the world. Songs are grouped according to months of the calendar and are accompanied by information on specific religious, national, or local customs. A bibliography is provided.

192. Nash, Grace C., and Janice Rapley. *Holidays and Special Days: A Sourcebook of Songs, Rhymes and Movement for Each Month of the Elementary School Year.* Van Nuys, CA: Alfred Publishing, 1988. 136pp.[P] Grades 1–6.

193. *Silverman, Jerry. *Holiday Songbook.* Pacific, MO: Mel Bay, 1992. 114pp. Arr. for piano and guitar. [P]
    This compilation of 47 songs spans every major holiday of the year and provides brief explanatory comments.

 Recording

194. *Holiday Songs Around the World.* Educational Activities, Freeport, NY, 1994. LP and videocassette, 30 min. Grades 1–6.
    In this recording child narrators giving information about holiday traditions in various countries are combined with groups singing various songs. Reproducible lyric sheets, activities, teacher's guide, and an audiocassette come with the video.

Local History
(*See also* Regions, States)

 Further Reading

195. *MacArthur, Margaret, with Gregory Sharrow. *The Vermont Heritage Songbook.* Middlebury, VT: The Vermont Folklife Center, c. 1994. 108pp. Arr. for guitar. Audiocassette available. [P]
    Written by MacArthur and local school children, this is a collection of 42 songs about people and events in Vermont history. An introduction providing suggestions for integrating music into the regular curriculum is included as well as a subject index.

196. *Webber, Mary. *Writing Ballads from Local Historical Legends.* Yarmouth, MA: Yarmouth Historical Society, 1989. (P.O. Box 107, Yarmouth, MA 04096) 36pp. [P] Grades 3+.
    This is an excellent guide on how to combine local history research with ballad writing.

Native Americans
(*See also* Regions)

 Articles

197. Ballard, Louis W. "Put American Indian Music in the Classroom," *Music Educators Journal* 56 (March 1970): 38–45. Grades 4+.
   Ballard provides background information on music of Native Americans, with specific examples from Papago, Kiowa, and Sioux traditions. Examples have melody, vocables/words, and drumbeats.

198. *Campbell, Patricia Shehan. "Conversations with David P. McAllester on Navajo Music," *Music Educators Journal* (July 1994): 17–23. Grades 5+.
   In this interview a noted ethnomusicologist explores the social and historical context of Navajo music. A map and lesson plan for a song—containing the melody and words—are also provided.

199. ———. "Native Americans of the Southwest," in *Multicultural Perspectives in Music Education*, edited by William M. Anderson and Patricia Shehan Campbell, 33–47. Reston, VA: Music Educators National Conference, 1989. Grades 5+.
   Background notes as well as four detailed lesson plans (one for making a drum and rattle) for teaching the music of Southwest Indians are given here.

200. McAllester, David P., and Edwin Schupman. "Teaching the Music of the American Indians," in *Teaching Music with a Multicultural Approach*, edited by William M. Anderson, 27–44. Reston, VA: Music Educators National Conference, 1991. Grades 6+.
   These ethnomusicologists present information on the diverse characteristics of the philosophy and history of American Indian music as well as lesson plans for understanding and performing a southern plains round dance and the Hopi song "Mos', Mos'!" A bibliography, discography, and filmography are provided.

 Books

201. Ballard, Louis W. *American Indian Music for the Classroom: Teachers Guide*. Phoenix, AZ: Canyon Records, 1973. 88pp.
   This resource on American Indian music includes songs, games, and dances from various Indian cultures. It contains 4 recordings, 20 photographs, 22 songsheets, and a bibliography.

202. Glass, Paul. *Songs and Stories of the North American Indians*. New York: Grosset & Dunlap, 1968. 61pp. [P]
   This is a collection of stories and 31 songs of the Yuma, Mandan and Teton Sioux, Pawnee, and Papago Indian tribes, including a capsule history of each tribe. Simple musical accompaniment with drumbeat notations is provided along with a brief explanation of each song's significance in tribal customs.

203. Tooze, Ruth, and Beatrice Perham Krone. *Literature and Music As Resources for Social Studies*. Englewood Cliffs, NJ: Prentice-Hall, 1955. 457pp.
   Although the children's book selections are dated, this is still a marvelous source of ideas for combining children's literature with social studies. Some songs are included. See Chapter 13, "The Indians in America." Bibliographies are provided.

 Recordings

For audiocassettes and compact discs of authentic performances of Native American music, one of the largest sources is *The Whole Folkways Catalog* from Smithsonian/Folkways Recordings, Center for Folklife Programs, 955 L'Enfant Plaza, Suite 2600, MRC 914, Washington, DC 20560. The catalog of Smithsonian/Folkways Recordings is also a valuable resource. Recordings are available in audiocassette or compact disc.

204. *Discovering American Indian Music*. Video Adventures, Irwindale, CA, 1982. videocassette, color. Grades 3–8.
   This film examines several kinds of Native American music and features instruments, singing, dancing, and costumes.

205. *Teaching the Music of the American Indian*. Music Educators National Conference, Reston, VA, c. 1991. videocassette, 37 min.
   Ethnomusicologists David P. McAllester and Edwin Schupman discuss the role of music education in multicultural education and explore resources available for teaching the music of Native Americans. Music examples and a teacher's guide are provided.

 Further Reading

206. McAllester, David P. "North America/Native America," in *Worlds of Music: An Introduction to the Music of the World's Peoples*, edited by Jeff Todd Titon, James T. Koetting, David P. McAllester, David B. Reck, and Mark Slobin, 12–64. New York: Schirmer Books, 1984.
   This is an excellent source for in-depth information on the music and culture of the Sioux and Navaho. It also includes plans

for making a cow-horn rattle and a water drum. A bibliography and discography are provided.

Occupations
(*See also* Regions)

General

 Article

207. Daniels, Elva S. "Great American Work Songs," *Instructor* 92, no. 7 (March 1983): 55–59, 62-63. Grades K–6.
    This teacher's guide looks at work songs of sailors, loggers, coal miners, and other laborers from the 1800s. Classroom activities along with words and music for seven songs are given including: "Cape Cod Shanty"; "The Jam on Gerry's Rocks"; "Corn-Husking Song"; "Cotton Needs Pickin'"; "Big Corral"; "Down, Down in a Coal Mine"; and "Hammer on the MD."

 Book

208. Silverman, Jerry. *Work Songs*. New York: Chelsea House, c. 1994. 64pp. Arr. for piano and guitar. [P] Grades 5+.
    This anthology presents 29 songs about work and famous laborers from the African American folk tradition.

 Recordings

209. *American Industrial Ballads*. Performed by Pete Seeger. Smithsonian Folkways 40058, Washington, DC, 1992. audiocassette and compact disc. Grades 5+.
    Descriptive notes with lyrics are provided for this recording. Titles include: "Peg and Awl"; "Blind Fiddler"; "Buffalo Skinners"; "Eight-Hour Day"; "Hard Times in the Mill"; "Roll Down the Line"; "Hayseed Like Me"; "Farmer Is the Man"; "Come All You Hardy Miners"; "He Lies in the American Land"; "Casey Jones"; "Let Them Wear Their Watches Fine"; "Cotton Mill Colic"; "Seven Cent Cotton and Forty Cent Meat"; "Mill Mother's Lament"; "Fare Ye Well, Old Ely Branch"; "Beans, Bacon and Gravy"; "Death of Harry Simms"; "Winnsboro Cotton Mill Blues"; "Ballad of Barney Graham"; "My Children Are Seven in Number"; "Raggedy"; "Sixty Per Cent"; and "Pittsburgh Town."

210. *Who Built America: American History Through Its Folksongs*. Performed by Bill Bonyun. Smithsonian/Folkways 07542, Washington, DC. audiocassette and compact disc. Grades 3–6.

Descriptive notes with lyrics are provided for this recording. Titles include: "Waly, Waly"; "Green Mountain Boys"; "Erie Canal"; "Shoot the Buffalo"; "Santy Anno"; "Happiness Song"; "My Government Claim"; "The Praties"; "Drill Ye Tarriers"; "Auction Block"; "Boll Weevil"; "Chisholm Trail"; "Jesse James"; "Mi Chaera"; "Schulf Mine Kind"; "Salangadou"; "Kleine Jonges"; and "So Long, Been Good to Know You."

211. *Working and Union*. Performed by Keith McNeil and Rusty McNeil. WEM Records, 1989. (16230 Van Buren Boulevard, Riverside, CA 92504) 2 audiocassettes, 90 min. Grades 5+.

A collection of 36 songs and narration that relate to the labor movement and unions in the United States from the 1860s to the 1930s are presented in this recording. Songs presented include: "Weave Room Blues"; "Ten and Nine"; "Hard Times in the Mill"; "Work of the Weavers"; "Ballad of Springhill"; "Blind Fiddler"; "Peg and Awl"; "Weary Cutters"; "Blow the Man Down"; "Pat Works on the Railway"; "Royal Telephone"; "Farmer Is the Man"; "In My Merry Oldsmobile"; "Solidarity Forever"; "Storm the Fort"; "Eight-Hour Day"; "My Sweetheart's a Mule in the Mines"; "Joe Hill"; "The Death of Mother Jones"; "Cotton Mill Girls"; "Ballad of Dead Girls"; "I.L.G.W.U."; "I Ain't Got No Home"; "We Shall Not Be Moved"; "Which Side Are You On?"; "Sit Down"; "The CIO Is Bigger Than It Used to Be"; "The Yablonski Murder"; "Buddy Won't You Roll Down the Line"; "Kumbaya"; "Nosotros Venceremos"; "Huelga"; "Niños Campesinos"; "My Old Man"; "Automation"; and "Aragon Mill." A booklet is included.

♪ *Further Sources of Songs*

212. Fowke, Edith, and Joe Glazer. *Songs of Work and Protest*. New York: Dover Publications, 1973. 209pp. Arr. for piano. [P]

One hundred songs, including union songs, songs of miners, mill workers, railroaders, farmers, abolitionists, and more are given here with historical notes. A bibliography and discography are provided.

213. Lomax, Alan. *The Folk Songs of North America*. Garden City, NY: Doubleday, 1960. 622pp. [P]

Marvelous anecdotes and background information are provided by one of America's leading folksong collectors. This anthology includes sections on soldiers, lumbermen, farmers, sailors, miners, railroaders, and cowboys.

214. Reid, Rob. *Children's Jukebox: A Subject Guide to Musical Recordings and Programming Ideas for Songsters Ages 1 to 12*. Chicago: American Library Association, 1995. 225pp.

    Arranged by subject, this select guide provides the titles for songs, along with the performing artist, title of recording, publication date, and distributor. Titles are listed alphabetically within each subject and a brief annotation describes the song and often includes programming ideas. See the section titled "Occupations." A subject index is included.

215. Seeger, Pete, and Bob Reiser. *Carry It On: The Story of America's Working People in Song and Picture*. New York: Simon & Schuster, 1985. 256pp. Arr. for guitar. [P]

    The experiences of working Americans, from the Revolution to the present, are reflected in the 80 songs and brief introductory notes gathered for this book.

 Further Reading

216. Foner, Philip S. *American Labor Songs of the 19th Century*. Urbana, IL: University of Illinois Press, 1975. 356pp.

    This work represents the most comprehensive source of information on the subject. Unfortunately, only the lyrics to songs are given.

217. Greenway, John. *American Folksongs of Protest*. 1953. Reprint, Philadelphia, PA: University of Pennsylvania Press, 1960. 348pp.

    The history of protest song in America is divided into chapters on songs of Afro-Americans, textile workers, miners, migrant workers, farmers, and others. Other chapters are devoted to individual song-makers such as Ella May Wiggins, Aunt Molly Jackson, Woody Guthrie, and Joe Glazer. Almost no music is provided. A discography and bibliography are included.

Cowboys

(*See also* American History: Western Expansion; Regions: Southwest, West; States)

 Pamphlet

218. Scott, John Anthony, and Laurence I. Seidman. "Songs of the American Cowboy," *Folksong in the Classroom* I, no. 4. (May 1981): 25pp. (P.O. Box 925, Sturbridge, MA 01566) Arr. for guitar. Grades 4+.

    This issue on folksong and history designed to aid teachers is devoted to the songs and background of the American cowboy.

Songs include: "The Cowboy's Lament"; "Goodbye Old Paint"; "Chisholm Trail"; "I Ride an Old Paint"; "Doney Girl"; "Git Along Little Dogies"; "Colorado Trail"; and "Down by the Brazos." Suggested activities and a bibliography are also given.

Recordings

219. *Cowboy Ballads*. Performed by Cisco Houston. Smithsonian/Folkways 02022, Washington, DC, 1952.

Descriptive notes with song lyrics as well as a glossary of cowboy terms are provided for this recording. Titles performed are: "Chisholm Trail"; "Diamond Joe"; "Old Paint"; "Little Joe, the Wrangler"; "Dying Cowboy"; "Stewball"; "Trouble in Mind"; "Sweet Betsy from Pike"; and "Tying a Knot in the Devil's Tail."

220. **Cowboy Songs*. Performed by Keith McNeil and Rusty McNeil. WEM Records, 1992. (16230 Van Buren Boulevard, Riverside, CA 92504) 2 audiocassettes and compact disc, 180 min.

The origins and uses of 50 traditional cowboy and ranch songs are described through narration and music. Titles include: "Bury Me on the Lone Prairie"; "Goodbye Old Paint"; "El Rancho Grande"; "Streets of Laredo"; "Home on the Range"; "El Alabado"; "La Sandunga"; "La Paloma"; "Spanish Is a Loving Tongue"; "The Cyclone Blues"; "The Farrows"; "Diamond Joe"; "What Was Your Name in the States?"; "Lakes of Ponchartrain"; "On the Lakes of the Poncho Plains"; "A Grant"; "A Prisoner for Life"; "Strawberry Roan"; "Blood on the Saddle"; "Zebra Dun"; "Miss Aldeo"; "Windy Bill"; "Texas Idol"; "Dreary, Dreary Life"; "Wild Rippling Water"; "Fair Lady of the Plains"; "Utah Carl"; "Cowboy Jack"; "Cowboy's Christmas Ball"; "Old Chisholm Trail"; "El Corrido De Kiansas"; "Doney Gal"; "The Cowboy"; "John Garner's Trail Herd"; "Juan Murray"; "Cowboy's Heaven"; "Railroad Corral"; "Old Man Rocking the Cradle"; "Get Along Little Dogies"; "Little Joe the Wrangler"; "Punchin' Dough"; "Hell in Texas"; "When the Work's All Done This Fall"; "Night Herding Song"; "Colorado Trail"; "Jim the Roper"; "Montana"; and "I'm Going to Leave Old Texas Now."

Further Sources of Songs

221. Fife, Austin E., and Alta S. Fife. *Cowboy and Western Songs: A Comprehensive Anthology*. 1969. Reprint, Ojai, CA: Creative Concepts, 1993. 372pp.

This book features 128 songs covering the frontier, travel, humor, work, good times, outlaws, and cowboy heroes. Each song is preceded by a brief description. A lexicon and bibliography are provided.

222. Reid, Rob. *Children's Jukebox: A Subject Guide to Musical Recordings and Programming Ideas for Songsters Ages 1 to 12*. Chicago: American Library Association, 1995. 225pp.

Arranged by subject, this select guide provides the titles for contemporary children's songs as well as the name of the performing artist, title of recording, publication date, and distributor. Titles are listed alphabetically within each subject. A brief annotation describes the song and often includes programming ideas. See the section titled "Cowboys/Cowgirls."

Farmers

(*See also* American History: Westward Expansion; Regions: New England, Southwest, West)

 ### Article

223. *Kracht, James B. "Perceptions of the Great Plains in Nineteenth Century Folk Song: Teaching About Place," *Journal of Geography* 88, no. 6 (November/December 1989): 206–12. Grades 4+.

Geography's impact on the lives of people and how it is reflected in folksong are discussed in this article. Teacher preparation material is provided along with a sample lesson plan with music and lyrics for four songs: "Home on the Range"; "Lane County Bachelor (Starving to Death on My Government Claim)"; "Dakota (Nebraska) Land"; and "The Kansas Fool." A bibliography is included.

 ### Pamphlet

224. Scott, John Anthony, and Laurence I. Seidman. "Farmers of the Plains and Prairies: Their Story in Song, 1850's-1880's." *Folksong in the Classroom* VI, no. 2 (winter 1986): 36–61. (P.O. Box 925, Sturbridge, MA 01566) Grades 4+.

This issue is dedicated to enriching the study of social studies, language arts, and the humanities for grades K–12 and features the lives, conditions, and experiences of farmers on the Great Plains as reflected in folksong. Along with introductory and background material, eight songs are provided: "Elanoy"; "Uncle Sam's Farm"; "Sow Took the Measles"; "Farmer's Curst Wife"; "Starving to Death on My Government Claim"; "Little Sod Shanty"; "Skip to My Lou"; and "Farmer Is the Man." Suggestions for follow-up activities are also given.

64 / SOCIAL STUDIES

 Recording

225. *An Almanac of New England Farm Songs.* Performed by Margaret MacArthur. (Available from Whetstone, P.O. Box 15, Malboro, VT 05344) audiocassette and compact disc.
    Titles in this recording include: "Our Forefather's Song"; "Maple Sweet"; "Shearing Day"; "The Vermont Farmer's Song"; "Old Mr. Grumble"; "Young Man Who Wouldn't Hoe Corn"; "Springfield Mountain"; "The Miller's Will"; "The Rolling Stone"; "Jones' Paring Bee"; and "Fifty Years Ago."

 Further Sources of Songs

226. Reid, Rob. *Children's Jukebox: A Subject Guide to Musical Recordings and Programming Ideas for Songsters Ages 1 to 12.* Chicago: American Library Association, 1995. 225pp.
    Arranged by subject, this select guide provides the titles for contemporary children's songs as well as the name of the performing artist, title of recording, publication date, and distributor. Titles are listed alphabetically within each subject. A brief annotation describes the song and often includes programming ideas. See the sections titled "Farms" and "Gardens." An index is provided.

227. *Sing the Earth: A Farming and Gardening Songbook.* Pittsboro, NC: Carolina Farm Stewardship Association (Route #2, Box 161-R, Pittsboro, NC 27312) 64pp. Arr. for guitar. [P] Grades 1–6.
    This songbook provides both traditional and contemporary folksongs about farming and gardening.

 Further Reading

228. Greenway, John. *American Folksongs of Protest.* Philadelphia, PA: University of Pennsylvania Press, 1960. 348pp.
    The history of protest song in America is divided in this book into chapters on songs of African Americans, textile workers, miners, migrant workers, farmers, and others. Almost no music is included. See Chapter 6, "Songs of the Farmers," for a good discussion on the subject. A discography and bibliography are included.

Lumbermen

(*See also* Regions: New England; States: Maine, Michigan)

 Pamphlet

229. Scott, John A., and Laurence I. Seidman. "Lumbering—Cutting Down the White Pine: The Shantyboys and the White River Men," *Folksong in the Classroom* V, no. 2 (winter 1985): 31–55. (P.O. Box 925, Sturbridge, MA 01566) Arr. for guitar. Grades 4+.

The songs of the lumbermen provide an extraordinary record of the daily life of American working men and express the joy and the challenge, as well as the tragedy, of the frontier experience. Songs in this resource are accompanied by excellent background notes, a section on shantyboys' words that have enriched our language, and follow-up activities. Titles include: "Lumberman's Alphabet"; "The Shantyman's Life"; "Les Raftsmen"; "Peter Emberly"; "Once More A-Lumbering Go"; "The Shantyboy and the Farmer's Son"; "Wild Colonial Boy"; "Little Brown Bulls"; "Michigan-I-O"; and "Jam on Gerry's Rocks." A bibliography and discography are included.

 Recording

230. *Timber-r-r! Folksongs and Ballads of the Lumberjacks*. Performed by Paul Clayton. Riverside Folklore Series, RLP 12-648. 195X. LP.

Descriptive notes with lyrics are provided in this recording. Titles include: "Lumberman"; "Alphabet"; "Jam on Gerry's Rock"; "Little Brown Bulls"; "Hanging Limb"; "James Whalen"; "Wild Mustard River"; "Banks of the Little Eau Plaine"; "Canaday"; "Jack Haggerty"; "Blue Mountain Lake"; "Backwoodsman"; "Lost Jimmy Whelan"; "Peter Amberly"; "Harry Bail"; and "Jolly Shantyboys."

 Further Sources of Songs

231. Barry, Phillips. *The Maine Woods Songster*. Cambridge, MA: Harvard University Press, 1939. 102pp.

As an early collector of New England folksong, Barry offers 50 songs, and ballads popular in the lumbercamps of the northeast.

232. Doerflinger, William Main. *Songs of the Sailor and Lumberman*. 1951. Reprint, New York: Macmillan, 1972. 374pp. (Originally titled *Shantymen and Shantyboys*)

Sixty-nine songs and ballads collected from the American and Canadian lumbermen are given here. Brief notes about the singers and the songs preface each piece. Of particular interest is Section VIII, "The Shantyboy's Life." A bibliography is included.

Mill (Textile) Workers

(*See also* Regions: New England, South; States)

♪ Books

233. Alloy, Evelyn. *Working Women's Music: The Songs and Struggles of Women in the Cotton Mills, Textile Plants and Needle Trades.* Somerville, MA: The New England Free Press, 1976. 44pp. Arr. for guitar. [P]

    Alloy presents 38 songs, with good notes and background information, that resulted from life in the New England mills, immigration, labor unrest, and the southern mill tradition.

234. Douglas, Jim. *From Farm to Factory: The Story of the New England Textile Industry in Song.* Sturbridge, MA: The Pedlar Press, 1987. (53 Whittemore Road, Sturbridge, MA 01566) 66pp. [P]

    This regional study contains 28 songs, with introductory material and song notes, that detail the development of the textile industry in New England from the colonial period to the twentieth century. A bibliography is included.

♪ Pamphlet

235. *Douglas, Jim, and John Anthony Scott. "The New England Textile Industry Through Its Songs," *Folksong in the Classroom* XIII, no. 3 (spring 1993): 10–28. (P.O. Box 925, Sturbridge, MA 01566) Arr. for guitar. Grades 5+. [ED 391731]

    This issue of this newsletter for teachers of English, history, music, and the humanities focuses on songs that document the rise and passing of the New England textile industry. An extensive introduction and notes provide context for the following songs: "A Sweet Country Life"; "Song of the Factory Girl"; "Pity Me, My Darling"; "The Lowell Factory Girl"; "Captain Kidd"; "Lord Lovell"; "The Burning of the Granite Mill"; "Deirin Dé"; "In the Good Old Picket Line"; "Bread and Roses"; and "Hard Times in the Mill." Suggested activities are included as well as a bibliography.

♪ Recording

236. *Cottonmill Girls.* Performed by Alex Demas. (Available from Bookstore, Lowell National Historical Park, Lowell, Massachusetts) 1986. audiocassette.

    Titles include: "A Weaver's Life"; "I Cannot Be a Slave"; "The Mills of Marble"; "Cottonmill Girls"; "No Irish Need Apply"; "Bread and Roses"; "Weaveroom Blues"; "Boxes of Bobbins"; "Babies in the Mill"; and "Aragon Mill."

Further Reading

237. Greenway, John. *American Folksongs of Protest*. 1953. Reprint, Philadelphia: University of Pennsylvania Press, 1960. 348pp.

    The history of protest song in America is divided into chapters on songs of African Americans, textile workers, miners, migrant workers, farmers, and others. Almost no music is provided. See chapter 3, "Songs of Textile Workers," for a good discussion of the subject. A discography and bibliography are included.

238. Minton, John. "The Southern Textile Song Tradition Reconsidered," in *Songs About Work, Essays in Occupational Cultures for Richard A. Reuss*, edited by Archie Green. Bloomington, IN: Folklore Institute, Indiana University Press, 1993.

    Minton reviews the southern tradition of mill songs and how humor has been used to help deal with hard times.

Miners

(*See also* American History: Gold Rush; Regions: South, Southwest; States: Pennsylvania)

 Pamphlet

239. Scott, John Anthony, and Laurence I. Seidman. "Mine, Mill and Tunnel Workers, 1877–1932," *Folksong in the Classroom* XI, no. 2 (winter 1991): 3–29. (P.O. Box 925, Sturbridge, MA 01566) Arr. for guitar. Grades 5+. [ED 340627]

    This issue of a resource for teachers was created by two teachers with extensive experience using folksongs in the classroom. It offers extensive introductory and background notes and eight songs of industrial workers that take students into the heart of working peoples' experiences. Titles include: "The Blantyre Explosion"; "Dark As a Dungeon"; "Bread and Roses"; "The Johnston Flood"; "Solidarity"; "John Henry of Hawk's Nest"; "Ragged and Dirty Blues"; and "The Death of Mother Jones." A bibliography is included.

 Recordings

240. *Come All You Coal Miners*. Rounder Records 4005, 1973. (1 Camp Street, Cambridge, MA 02140). LP.

    Performed by their composers, these songs were recorded at an Appalachian Music Workshop held at the Highlander Center in New Market, TN, in October 1972. Titles provided are: "Black Lung Blues"; "Black Lung"; "Don't You Want to Go to That Land"; "Cold

Blooded Murder"; "Come All You Coal Miners"; "Both Lungs Is Broke Down"; "Dreadful Memories"; "Clay County Miner"; "The N & W Train Don't Stop Here No More"; "That 25 Cents That You Paid"; and "Mannington Mine Disaster."

241. *Down in a Coal Mine.* Performed by Joe Glazer. Collector Records, 1923. (Suite 201, 8422 Georgia Ave., Silver Spring, MD 20910). LP.

Songs in this recording are: "Down in a Coal Mine"; "My Sweetheart's the Mule in the Mines"; "Young Lady Who Married a Mule Driver"; "When the Breaker Starts up Full Time"; "Jolly Wee Miner Men"; "Death of Mother Jones"; "Old Miner's Refrain"; "Miner's Life"; "Ludlow Massacre"; "Company Store"; "Sixteen Tons"; "Which Side Are You On?"; "Union Man"; "Drill Man Blues"; and "Coal Miner's Heaven."

 Further Reading

242. Greenway, John. *American Folksongs of Protest*. 1953. Reprint, Philadelphia: University of Pennsylvania Press, 1960. 348pp.

The history of protest song in America is divided into chapters on songs of African Americans, textile workers, miners, migrant workers, farmers, and others. Almost no music is provided. See chapter 4, "Songs of the Miners," for a good discussion of the subject. A discography and bibliography are included.

243. Yurchenco, Henrietta. "Trouble in the Mines: A History in Song and Story by Women of Appalachia," *American Music* 9, no. 2 (summer 1991): 209–24.

This article discusses the role of women in the mines of Appalachia in the twentieth century and provides special emphasis on the lives and work of songwriting activists such as Aunt Molly Jackson, Sarah Ogan Gunning, Florence Reese, and Hazel Dickens.

Sailors

(*See also* Occupations: Whalers; Transportation: Ships)

Pamphlet

244. Scott, John Anthony, and Laurence I. Seidman. "Songs of the Sea: Chanties, Fo'c'sle and Fishing Songs," *Folksong in the Classroom* IV, no. 2 (winter 1984): 31–52. (P.O. Box 925, Sturbridge, MA 01566) Arr. for guitar. Grades 4+. [ED 273507]

Shanties (work songs) and other songs at sea played an important role for work while fo'c'sle (off-duty) songs provided entertainment for sailors. Titles on this recording include: "Boney";

"Haul Away Joe"; "Lowlands"; "Blood Red Roses"; "Shenandoah"; "Bound for the Rio Grande"; "Henry Martin"; "Banks of Newfoundland"; "Lord Franklin"; "Boston Come All Ye"; and "A Trip to the Grand Banks." Extensive background notes, introductory notes, and follow-up teaching ideas are provided as well as a bibliography.

♪ Recordings

245. *Fo'c'sle Songs and Shanties*. Performed by Paul Clayton and the Fo'c'sle Singers. Smithsonian/Folkways 02429, Washington, DC, 1959. audiocassette and compact disc.

This recording includes descriptive notes with lyrics. Songs performed are: "Ratcliffe Highway"; "Rio Grande"; "Haul on the Bowline"; "Maggie May"; "Leave Her Johnny"; "Paddy Lay Back"; "Fire Down Below"; "A Hundred Years Ago"; "Santy Anno"; "Captain Nipper"; "Hanging Johnny"; "Banks of Sacramento"; and "Won't You Go My Way?"

246. **Roll and Go, The Shantyman's Day Aboard a Yankee Clipper*. Performed by Bill Bonyun. Heirloom Records 504. (Route 2, Wiscasset, ME 04518) audiocassette.

Through both narrative and song, a day in the life of a shantyman is told. A teacher's guide is provided. Songs performed are: "Paddy Get Back"; "Cherrily Man"; "Bust and Bend Her"; "Johnny Come Down to Hilo"; "England Old Ireland"; "Blow the Man Down"; "Tommy's Gone to Hilo"; "Haul Away My Rosey"; "Hilly Riley"; "Shenandoah"; "South Australia"; "Boney"; "Drunken Sailor"; "Haul on the Bowline"; "Haul Away Joe"; "Round the Bay of Mexico"; "Banks of Newfoundland"; "Jolly Roving Tar"; "First Voyage"; "Adieu to Maimuna"; "Let Go the Reefy Tackle"; and "Paddy Doyle."

247. *Songs of the Sea*. Performed by Alan Mills and the Shanty Men. Smithsonian/Folkways 02312, Washington, DC, 1957.

This recording includes descriptive notes with lyrics and a study guide. Songs performed are: "Rio Grande"; "Haul Away Joe"; "Sally Brown"; "Cherrily, Men"; "Johnny Boker"; "Paddy Doyle's Boots"; "Dead Horse"; "Salt Horse"; "A-Roving"; "Tom's Gone to Hilo"; "Johnny Come Down to Hilo"; "Ten Thousand Miles Away"; "Shenandoah"; "Billy Boy"; "Lowlands"; "Drunken Sailor"; "Blow, Boys, Blow"; "Blow the Man Down"; "Clear the Track, Let the Bullgine Run"; "Can't You Dance the Polka"; "A Long Time Ago"; "New Bedford Whalers"; "Fire Down Below"; "Sailor's Grave Boney Was a Warrior"; "Santy Anna"; "Home, Dearie, Home"; "Goodbye, Fare Ye Well"; "Hilo Somebody"; "Galloping Randy Dandy O"; and "Leave Her, Johnny."

248. *Steady As She Goes: Songs and Chanties from the Days of Commercial Sail.* Performed by Louis Killen, Jeff Warner, Gerret Warner, and John Benson. Collector Records, 1928, reprint 1977. LP.

Songs performed in this recording are: "Paddy Lay Back"; "Bold Riley"; "Rolling Down to Old Maui"; "Jolly Roving Tar"; "Topman and the Afterguard"; "Off to Sea Once More"; "Strike the Bell"; "Ship in Distress"; "Blow the Man Down"; "Coast of Peru"; "All for Me Grog"; "Shallow Brown"; "Bring 'Em Down"; and "Away Rio."

♪ Further Sources of Songs

249. Colcord, Joanna. *Songs of American Sailormen.* 1924. Reprint, New York: W. W. Norton, 1938. 212pp. (Originally published as *Roll and Go: Songs of American Sailormen*)

An important work, this book includes 109 songs, both shanties and fo'c'sle songs with background information on individual songs.

250. Doerflinger, William Main. *Songs of the Sailor and Lumberman.* 1951. Reprint, New York: Macmillan, 1972. 374pp. (Originally published as *Shantymen and Shantyboys*)

Half of this book contains songs that sailors sang aboard deep-water vessels, fishing schooners of the western North Atlantic, and in the West Indies trade. Both shanties (work songs) and songs of the forecastle are represented.

251. Harlow, Frederick Pease. *Chanteying Aboard American Ships.* Barre, MA: Barre Publishing, 1962. 250pp.

Harlow provides mainly shanties with good descriptions of their purpose, as well as a few whaling songs and general "sea songs."

252. Hugill, Stan. *Shanties from the Seven Seas.* 1971. Reprint, Mystic, CT: Mystic Seaport Museum, 1994. 416pp.

Unlike most other collectors of sailors' songs, Hugill was an authentic shantyman and is considered to be the authority on the subject.

Soldiers

(*See also* American History: American Revolution, Civil War, War of 1812, World War II, Vietnam)

253. Scott, John Anthony. "Songs of Soldiers," *Folksong in the Classroom* XI, no. 3 (spring 1991): 7–30. (P.O. Box 925, Sturbridge, MA 01566) Arr. for guitar. Grades 6+.

Songs about war and soldiering from the eighteenth, nineteenth, and twentieth centuries are included in this excellent teacher's resource, along with good background information on each song. Titles include: "How Stands the Glass Around"; "The Wars of High Germany"; "Bucking and Gagging"; "John Brown of Massachusetts"; "A Plaint"; "Virginia's Bloody Soil"; "Mademoiselle from Armentieres"; "Peat Bog Soldiers"; and "Where Have All the Flowers Gone?" A bibliography is included.

 Further Sources for Songs

254. Dolph, Edward Arthur. *Sound Off! Soldier Songs.* New York: Farrar & Rinehart, 1929. 620pp. Arr. for piano.
   A large compilation of American soldiers' songs, this work includes more than 300 songs from every war from the American Revolution to World War II. Brief notes preface each song.

Whalers
(*See also* Sailors)

 Pamphlet

255. *Scott, John A., and Laurence I. Seidman. "The Golden Age of Whaling in New England," *Folksong in the Classroom* II, no. 2 (February 1982): 29–45. (P.O. Box 925, Sturbridge, MA 01566) Arr. for guitar. Grades 4+.
   This excellent resource features songs that tell the story of the whaling industry through the following songs: "Greenland Whale Fisheries"; "Heave Away My Johnnies"; "The *Diamond*"; "Rolling Home"; "We'll Rant and We'll Roar"; and "Off to Sea Once More." Introductory notes and follow-up activities are provided, as well as a select bibliography of books on whaling for students and teachers.

 Recordings

256. *Songs of Yankee Whaling.* Performed by Bill Bonyun and chorus. American Heritage, 1960. LP.
   Produced in cooperation with American Heritage to supplement the book by the same title, this recording combines songs with narration to describe the whaling industry. Titles include: "Greenland Whale Fishery"; "The *Diamond*"; "Off to Sea Once More"; "Cold Coast of Greenland"; "Blow Ye Winds in the Morning"; "A Fitting Out"; "Rueben Ranzo"; "Cape Horn"; "Coast of Peru"; "Rio Grande"; "Jack Was Every Inch a Sailor"; "Ship in Distress"; "We'll Rant and We'll Roar"; "E Tau Hoa Here"; "Little Mohea"; "Sailor's Grave"; and "Rolling Home."

257. *Whaler Out of New Bedford, and Other Songs of the Whaling Era.* Performed by Ewan MacColl and Peggy Seeger. Smithsonian/Folkways 03850, Washington, DC. audiocassette and compact disc.

This recording reproduces the music score from a whaling film by the same name. Descriptive notes with lyrics are included. Songs performed are: "Fitting Out"; "Boney"; "The Bark Gay Head"; "Boston-Come-All-Ye"; "Coast of Peru"; "Mary Ann"; "Desolation"; "A Hundred Years on the Eastern Shore"; and "Homeward Bound."

 Further Sources of Songs

258. Huntington, Gale. *Songs the Whalemen Sang.* Barre, MA: Barre Publishing, 1964. 328pp.

Huntington scoured old logs and other manuscript sources from New England and published the songs he found. This collection includes songs about whaling, the sea and ships, sailors and women, New England folk and popular songs, and versions of British songs. A bibliography is provided.

Regions
(*See also* States)

General

 Further Sources of Songs

259. Lomax, John. *The Folk Songs of North America.* Garden City, NY: Doubleday, 1960. 623pp. Arr. for guitar and piano. [P]

One of America's foremost authorities on folksong provides wonderful anecdotes and commentary for 317 songs from the northern regions, southern mountains and backwoods, the West, and southern Black tradition. A bibliography and discography are included.

The Great Lakes

(*See also* American History: War of 1812;
Occupations: Sailors; Transportation: Ships; States)

 Recordings

260. **Folk Songs of the Great Lakes Region.* Performed by Lee Murdock. Kanesville, IL: Depot Recordings. (Depot Recordings, P.O. Box 11, Kanesville, IL 60144) audiocassette. Grades 5+.

This recording presents 13 traditional songs from the Great Lakes region and includes background information and classroom activities. Songs cover pioneer life, farming, lumbering, and shipping. Titles include: "The Erie Canal"; "Shenandoah"; "The Housewife's Lament"; "The Farmer Is the Man"; "The Lumberman's Alphabet"; "The *Persia*'s Crew"; and "The *Bigler*'s Crew." A teacher's guide and map are provided.

261. *Songs of the Great Lakes.* Collected by Edith Fowke. Smithsonian/Folkways 04018, Washington, DC, c. 1964.

Descriptive notes and song lyrics are provided with this recording. Titles include: "The *E. C. Roberts*"; "The *Maggie Hunter*"; "The *Dreadnaught*"; "James Bird"; "The *Fayette Brown*"; "The Loss of the *Antelope*"; "Homeward Bound"; "The *Cumberland's* Crew"; "The *Merrimac*"; "The Schooner *Persian's* Crew"; "The Wreck of the *Asia*"; and "The Trip of the *Bigler*."

The Great Plains

(*See also* American History: General, Westward Expansion;
Occupations: Farmers; Native American; States)

 Book

262. Garson, Eugenia. *The Laura Ingalls Wilder Songbook: Favorite Songs from the "Little House" Books.* 1968. Reprint, New York: HarperCollins Childrens Books, 1996. 169pp. Arr. for piano and guitar. Grades 4–7.

This is a compilation of the 62 songs and tunes Pa Ingalls played on his fiddle and Ma Ingalls sang to her family, as mentioned in the Little House series of books. It includes ballads, folksongs, dances, minstrel show tunes, old hymns, and gospel songs, with brief introductory notes.

74 / SOCIAL STUDIES

 Pamphlets

263. Kracht, James B. "Perceptions of the Great Plains in Nineteenth Century Folk Song: Teaching About Place," *Journal of Geography* 88, no. 6 (November/December 1989): 206–12. Grades 4+.
    This article illustrates how geography affects peoples' lives and how it is reflected in folksong. Teacher preparation material is provided along with a sample lesson plan that includes four songs: "Home on the Range"; "Lane County Bachelor (Starving to Death on My Government Claim)"; "Dakota (Nebraska) Land"; and "The Kansas Fool." A bibliography is provided.

264. *Scott, John A., and Laurence I. Seidman. "Farmers of the Plains and Prairies: Their Story in Song, 1850's-1880's," *Folksong in the Classroom* VI, no. 2 (winter 1986): 35–61. (P.O. Box 925, Sturbridge, MA 01566) Arr. for guitar. Grades 4+.
    This issue of a newsletter dedicated to enriching the study of social studies, language arts, and the humanities for grades K–12 features the lives, conditions, and experiences of farmers on the Great Plains as reflected in folksong. Introductory and background material as well as follow-up activities are provided. Titles include: "Elaine"; "Uncle Sam's Farm"; "Sow Took the Measles"; "Farmer's Crust Wife"; "Starving to Death on My Government Claim"; "Little Sod Shanty"; "Skip to My Low"; and "Farmer Is the Man." A bibliography and discography are provided.

 Recordings

265. *History Alive Through Music: Musical Memories of Laura Ingalls Wilder*. Hear and Learn Publications, Vancouver, WA, 1993. audiocassette, 35 min.
    This recording features performances of songs mentioned in the Little House series by Laura Ingalls Wilder, including: "Wait for the Wagon"; "Sweet By and By"; "Buffalo Gals"; "Pop Goes the Weasel"; and "The Girl I Left Behind Me." A 52-page booklet with sheet music and background information comes with the cassette.

266. *A Little Music on the Prairie: Music from the Books of Laura Ingalls Wilder*. Performed by Mary DesRosiers, Nat Hewitt, and Pete Sutherland. Red Branch 002. (P.O. Box 196, Harrisville, NH 03450) audiocassette and compact disc.
    This is a nice production of songs and tunes mentioned or quoted in the Little House series of books. Titles include: "Oh Susannah/Old Dan Tucker"; "Arkansas Traveller/Devil's Dream"; "Green Grows the Laurel"; "Oh Come Away"; "Gum Tree Canoe/The Juanita"; "Camptown Races"; "Barbara Allen"; "Billy Boy"; "Roll the Old Chariot Along"; "Long Time Traveling"; "Money Musk"; "Just a Song at Twilight"; "Angel Band"; "Dixie/Cindy"; and "Buffalo Gals."

New England

(*See also* American History: General; Occupations: Farmers, Sailors, Mill Workers, Whalers)

 Book

267. *Douglas, Jim. *Songs of New England: A Resource Book for Teachers*. Sturbridge, MA: Pedlar Press, 1992. (53 Whittemore Road, Sturbridge, MA 01566) 159pp. Arr. for guitar. [P]

> More than 60 songs are gathered here that tell the story of New England work and history from the early colonial period to the late nineteenth century. An excellent introduction provides background information on the role of song and discusses the use of song in the classroom. A topical guide and bibliography are included.

 Recordings

268. *An Almanac of New England Farm Songs*. Performed by Margaret MacArthur. (Available from Whetstone, P.O. Box 15, Marlboro, VT 05344) audiocassette and compact disc.

> Songs performed include: "Our Forefather's Song"; "Maple Sweet"; "Shearing Day"; "The Vermont Farmer's Song"; "Old Mr. Grumble"; "Young Man Who Wouldn't Hoe Corn"; "Springfield Mountain"; "The Miller's Will"; "Rolling Stone"; "Jones' Paring Bee"; and "Fifty Years Ago."

269. *A Peddler's Pack*. Performed by Jim Douglas. Smithsonian/Folkways 32319, Washington, DC. audiocassette and compact disc.

> This recording provides descriptive notes with lyrics to a variety of songs traditional in New England. Titles include: "In the Good Old Colony Days"; "Maple Sweet"; "Jennie Jenkins"; "Old Man Who Lived in the Woods"; "Plymouth Colony"; "The Connecticut Peddler"; "Cape Cod Girls"; "Rolling Home"; "Logger's Boast"; "Revolutionary Tea"; "The Deer Song"; and "Froggie Would A-Wooing Go."

270. *Yankee Legend*. Performed by Bill and Gene Bonyun. Heirloom Records. (Route 2, Wiscasset, ME 04518) LP.

> This recording contains a good selection of New England songs and narration. Songs provided are: "Young Man Who Wouldn't Hoe Corn"; "The Old Man in the Wood"; "Jennie Jenkins"; "The Golden Vanity"; "Father Abby's Will"; "The Connecticut Peddler"; "The Frog in the Spring"; "Katie Cruel"; "Johnny Has Gone for a Soldier"; "Lumberman's Alphabet"; and "Song of the Fishes." A teacher's guide with lyrics is included.

Further Sources of Songs

271. Flanders, Helen Harkness, and Margaret Olney. *Ancient Ballads Traditionally Sung in New England.* 4 vols. Philadelphia, PA: University of Pennsylvania Press, 1965.
    Each volume contains variants of Child ballads collected from New England. Child ballads are some of the oldest surviving ballads from oral tradition in the English language. They are named after the Harvard professor who collected them and their variants and published them with extensive commentary in a classic work, *The English and Scottish Popular Ballads.*

272. ———. *Ballads Migrant in New England.* 1953. Reprint, North Stratford, NH: Ayer, 1977. 248pp.
    This book presents 96 ballads—texts and melodies included—along with a running commentary describing the people who preserved the songs, the way they were collected, and a historical background.

273. Linscott, Eloise Hubbard. *Folk Songs of Old New England.* 1939. Reprint, New York: Dover, 1993. 368pp. Arr. for piano.
    This collection provides music and comments on singing games, country dances (with directions and calls), shanties and fo'c'sle songs, ballads, folksongs, and ditties.

The South

 (*See also* African American; American History: General, Civil War, Slavery; Occupations: Farmers, Mill Workers, Miners; Transportation: Riverboats; States)

Article

274. McCullough-Brabson, Ellen, Patricia Shehan Campbell, and James Standifer. "Southern Appalachian Mountains," in *Multicultural Perspectives in Music Education*, edited by William M. Anderson, 9–32. Music Educators National Conference, 1989. Grades 5+.
    This is a discussion of southern Appalachian music by several ethnomusicologists featuring its traditions and characteristics. Included are short lesson plans on ballads, dulcimers, storytelling, dance, the making and use of a wooden rhythm dancing toy (the limberjack), and call and response songs. Songs include: "Mr. Frog Went A-Courtin'"; "The Wraggle Taggle Gypsies"; "Old Joe Clark"; and "Every Night When the Sun Goes Down." Suggestions are provided for integrating music with social studies, geography, history, and visual and performing arts classes.

♪ Recordings

275. *American Patchwork: Appalachian Journey*. PBS Home Video 300, 1990. (Distributed by Pacific Arts, Beverly Hills, CA) videocassette, 60 min., color.
   This video traces the development of southern mountain music and includes examples of mountain fiddling, banjo-playing, clogging (dance), ballad singing, and country music.

276. *Echoes of America*. Landmark Film, Falls Church, VA, 1991. videocassette, 52 min., color.
   This video explores the banjo and its history: how it was brought to American by African slaves, and the development of various styles. Performances and interviews with musicians Odell Thompson, Bill Munroe, Bill Keith, and Pete Seeger are included.

277. *Music in the Old Time Way: Traditional Music and Musicians from the Southern Appalachians*. Moving Image Productions, 1988. videocassette, 60 min.
   The development of "old-timey" acoustic, string band music is traced in this video, along with performances by various traditional musicians.

278. *Tipple, Loom & Rail: Songs of the Industrialization of the South*. Performed by Mike Seeger. Smithsonian/Folkways 05273, Washington, DC, 1966. audiocassette and compact disc.
   Descriptive notes and lyrics are included in this recording. Songs featured are: "A Factory Girl"; "Coal Creek Troubles"; "Tribute to Edward Lewis"; "Come All You Coal Miners"; "Miner's Blues"; "Harlan County Blues"; "Cotton Mill Blues"; "Reckless Motorman"; "New Market Wreck"; "Cotton Mill Colic"; "Virginian Strike of '23"; "Roane County Strike at Harriman, Tenn."; "Hard Working Miner"; "Hard Times in These Mines"; "Spinning Room Blues"; and "John Henry."

 Further Sources for Songs

279. Sharp, Cecil J., and Maud Karpeles. *English Folk Songs from the Southern Appalachians*. vol. 2. London: Oxford University Press, 1932. 476pp.
   Cecil Sharp, an English folksong collector, helped dispel the idea that oral preservation of ballads was a dead art in the twentieth century when he documented hundreds of ballads alive and well among the hill and mountain residents of the Southern Appalachians. This collection contains 273 ballads, songs, nursery songs, and play-party games whose origins can be traced to old England.

The Southwest

(*See also* American History: General, Native American,
Westward Expansion; Occupations: Cowboys; States;
World Cultures: Latin America)

Further Sources for Songs

280. Moore, Ethel, and Chauncy O. Moore. *Ballads and Folksongs of the Southwest*. Norman, OK: University of Oklahoma Press, 1964. 414pp.
    This is a collection of 194 songs and includes versions of British Child ballads and songs as well as songs of American origin. Brief background notes accompany the songs, and a bibliography is provided.

281. Swan, Howard. *Music in the Southwest, 1825-1950*. 1952. Reprint, New York: Da Capo Press, 1977. 316pp.
    This collection includes songs of the Mormons and miners as well as some Native American and Spanish music.

282. Van Stone, Mary. *Spanish Folk Songs of the Southwest*. 1928. Reprint, Academy Guild Press, 1963. 44pp. Arr. for piano.
    Twenty-five songs in Spanish are presented here, with English translations, that came out of the Spanish southwestern experience.

The West

(*See also* American History: General, Gold Rush,
Western Expansion; Native American;
Occupations: Cowboys; States)

Book

283. *Silber, Irwin, and Earl Robinson. *Songs of the Great American West*. 1967. Reprint, New York: Dover, 1995. 352pp.
    The social and historical background for 89 songs is presented in this work. Topics include cowboys, the gold rush, the Mexican-American conflict, farmers, and outlaws. A bibliography and discography are included.

Further Sources of Songs

284. Lingenfelter, Richard E., Richard A. Dwyer, and David Cohen. *Songs of the American West*. Los Angeles: University of California Press, 1968. 595pp. Arr. for guitar.

This is an extensive collection of songs about overland travel, travel 'round the Horn, railroads, mining, Mormons, Indian attacks, cowboys, and farming the prairie. Unfortunately, there are no descriptive notes.

285. *Silverman, Jerry. *Songs of the Western Frontier*. Pacific, MO: Mel Bay Publications, 1992. 111pp. Arr. for piano and guitar. [P]
Silverman, a prolific compiler of folksong anthologies, has put together a selection of cowboy songs, songs of the California gold rush, and songs from plains pioneers.

States
(*See also* Regions)

 Book

286. Silverman, Jerry. *Songs of the American People*. Pacific, MO: Mel Bay Publications, 1993. 235pp. Arr. for piano and guitar. [P]
This anthology presents two folksongs for every state with a brief note. Each song says something about the people or history of the state.
Further Sources of Songs: State Folksong Collections. These generally contain information about the history of songs collected within a state.

Alabama

287. Arnold, Byron. *Folksongs of Alabama*. Tuscaloosa, AL: University of Alabama Press, 1950.

288. Courlander, Harold. *Negro Songs from Alabama*. New York: Oak Publications, 1963. [P]

289. *Ring Games of Alabama*. Smithsonian/Folkways, Washington, DC, 1953. audiocassette and compact disc.
Descriptive notes are provided in this recording as well as lyrics for ring games, line games, and play party songs. Titles include: "Mary Mack"; "Bob a Needle"; "Watch That Lady"; "Old Lady Sally Wants to Jump"; "Loop de Loo"; "Green, Green Rocky Road"; "Rosie, Darling Rosie"; "I Must See"; "Bluebird, Bluebird"; "May Go 'Round the Needle"; "Stopping on the Window"; and "Charlie over the Ocean."

California

290. Arlen, Karen W. *They Came Singing: Songs from California's History.* 4th ed. Oakland, CA: Calicanto Associates, 1996. 110pp. compact disc included.
    This is a musicbook of songs that tell the story of California and includes songs of Native Americans, the Spanish and Mexican influence (with singable translations), the days of sail, and the gold rush. A bibliography and a map are provided.

Connecticut

291. Douglas, Jim. *Contentment, or, The Compleat Nutmeg-State Songster: 1760–1840.* Sturbridge, MA: Pedlar Press, 1984. (53 Whittemore Road, Sturbridge, MA 01566) [P]

Florida

292. Morris, Alton C. *Folksongs of Florida.* 1950. Reprint, Orlando, FL: University of Florida Press, 1990.

Idaho

293. *Folk Songs of Idaho and Utah.* Performed by Rosalie Sorrels. Smithsonian/Folkways 05343, Washington, DC, 1961. audiocassette and compact disc.
    Descriptive notes and lyrics are provided with this recording, which includes titles such as: "Lynman's Hymn"; "Brigham Young"; "Winter Song"; "Death of Kathy Fiscus"; "I'll Give You My Story"; "The Girl That Played Injun with Me"; "Utah's Dixie"; "Empty Cots in the Bunkhouse Tonight"; "Tying Knots in the Devil's Tail"; "The Fox"; "Way Out in Idaho"; "My Last Cigar"; "Wreck of Old Number Nine"; "House Carpenter"; "Wild Colonial Boy"; "I Left My Baby"; and "Philadelphia Lawyer."

Illinois

294. McIntosh, David. *Folk Songs and Singing Games of the Illinois Ozarks.* Carbondale, IL: Southern Illinois University Press, 1974.

Indiana

295. Brewster, Paul. *Ballads and Songs of Indiana*. 1940. Reprint, New York: Folklorica, 1981.

296. *Singing Indiana History: A Musical Resource Guide for Teachers*. Riverside Productions, Delphi, IN, 1992. audiocassette.
    This resource provides three cassettes presenting songs from and about Indiana as performed by professional artists and school children. An accompanying 229-page notebook by Martha Chrisman Riley of songs, poems, and stories covers the following topics: Indiana state songs; native tribes of Indiana; French voyagers and settlers; pioneer days; underground railroad and Civil War; farming; rivers and railroads; James Whitcomb Riley (poet); parlor music and tin pan alley; Hoagy Carmichael and Cole Porter; blues, ragtime, and jazz; university fight songs; and Indiana musicians, 1950-1990. A bibliography is included.

297. Wolford, Leah Jackson. *The Play-Party in Indiana*. Edited and revised by W. Edson Richmond and William Tillson. Publication 20, no. 2. Indianapolis, IN: Indiana Historical Society, 1959.

Kentucky

298. Fuson, Henry H. *Ballads of the Kentucky Highlands*. London: Mitre Press, 1931.

299. McGill, Josephine. *Folk Songs of the Kentucky Mountains*. New York: Boosey, 1917.

300. Thomas, Jean. *Ballad Makin' in the Mountains of Kentucky*. New York: Henry Holt, 1939.

301. ———. *Devil's Ditties*. Chicago: W. W. Hatfield, 1931.

Louisiana

302. Whitefield, Irene. *Louisiana French Folk Songs*. 1939. Reprint, New York: Dover, 1969.

Maine

303. Barry, Phillips. *The Maine Woods Songster*. Cambridge, MA: Harvard University Press, 1939.

304. Barry, Phillips, Fannie Hardy Eckstorm, and Mary Winslow Smyth. *British Ballads from Maine*. 1929. Reprint, New York: Da Capo Press, 1982.

305. Eckstorm, Fannie, and Mary Winslow Smyth. *Minstrelsy of Maine*. Boston: Houghton Mifflin, 1927.

306. *Folk Songs of Maine*. Performed by Sandy Ives. Smithsonian/Folkways 05323, Washington, DC. audiocassette and compact disc.
     Descriptive notes and lyrics are included with this recording. Titles performed are: "Lovewell's Fight"; "Aroostook War Song"; "Miramichi Fire"; "Santy Anna"; "Cumberland's Crew"; "Stately Southerner"; "Shanty Boys"; "Trip to the Grand Banks"; "Boys of the Island"; "Sally Brown"; "Old Beggar Man"; "Tittery Nan"; and "Peter Emberly."

Maryland

307. Carey, George G. *Maryland Folk Legends and Folk Songs*. Cambridge, MD: Tidewater, 1971.

Massachusetts

308. *Bay State Ballads*. Performed by Paul Clayton. Smithsonian Folkways 02106, Washington, DC, 1970. audiocassette and compact disc.
     Descriptive notes with lyrics are provided with this recording which includes titles such as: "Cape Cod Girls"; "Huzza for Commodore Rogers"; "The Ocean Rover"; "Blow the Man Down"; "Come All Ye Shipmates"; "Whiskey Johnny"; "Seaman's Grave"; "Springfield Mountain"; "Bailiff's Daughter of Islington"; "Old Soldier"; "Polly Van"; "The Embargo"; "Bachelor's Hall"; and "Around the Ingals Blazing."

Michigan

309. Gardner, Emelyn E., and Geraldine J. Chickering. *Ballads and Songs of Southern Michigan*. Ann Arbor, MI: University of Michigan Press, 1939.

310. Rickaby, Franz. *Ballads and Songs of the Shantyboy*. Cambridge, MA: Harvard University Press, 1926.

Mississippi

311. Hudson, Arthur Palmer. *Folksongs of Mississippi*. Chapel Hill, NC: University of North Carolina Press, 1936.

Missouri

312. Belden, H. M. *Ballads and Songs Collected by the Missouri Folklore Society*. Columbia, MO: University of Missouri, 1955.

313. Randolph, Vance. *Ozark Folksongs*. 4 vols. edited by Norm Cohen. 1946–1947. Reprint, Champaign, IL: University of Illinois Press, 1982.

314. *Missouri Folk Songs*. Performed by Loman D. Cansler. Smithsonian/Folkways 05324, Washington, DC. audiocassette and compact disc.
    Descriptive notes with lyrics are provided with this recording. Titles include: "Sally"; "Arthur Clyde"; "When I Went for to Take My Leave"; "Judgement Day"; "The Lover's Quarrel"; "The Two Sisters"; "Kickin' Maude"; "Charles Giteau"; "I Told 'Em Not to Grieve After Me"; "Joe Bowers"; "Housekeeper's Complaint"; "What Is a Home Without Love?"; "The Blue and the Gray"; and "Far Away."

New Hampshire

315. Warner, Anne. *Traditional American Folk Songs from the Anne and Frank Warner Collection*. New York: Syracuse University Press, 1984.

New Mexico

316. Robb, John. *Hispanic Folk Songs of New Mexico*. 1953. Reprint, Albuquerque, NM: University of New Mexico Press, 1978.

317. Van Stone, Mary. *Spanish Folk Songs of New Mexico*. Chicago, IL: Ralph F. Seymour, 1928.

New York

318. Cazden, Norman. *Folk Songs of the Catskills*. Albany, NY: State University of New York Press, 1982.

319. Warner, Anne. *Traditional American Folk Songs from the Anne and Frank Warner Collection*. New York: Syracuse University Press, 1984.

320. *Body, Boots, & Britches*. Performed by Golden Eagle String Band. Smithsonian/Folkways 32317, Washington, DC, 1982. audiocassette and compact disc.

    Descriptive notes and lyrics are provided with this recording. Titles include: "Captain Kidd"; "A Life on the Raging Canal"; "Napolean"; "Wrapped in Red Flannels"; "Ballad of Henry Green"; "Buggery Boo"; "Derby Ram"; "McKinley"; "Mermaid"; "I've Travelled All Around This World"; "Tebo"; "Battle of Plattsburg"; and "New York Fiddle Medley."

321. *Fifty Sail on Newburgh Bay*. Performed by Pete Seeger and Ed Reneham. Smithsonian/Folkways 05257, Washington, DC. audiocassette and compact disc.

    This recording presents descriptive notes and lyrics for traditional and contemporary songs from the Hudson River Valley. Titles performed include: "Kyowagena"; "Fifty Sail on Newburgh Bay"; "Burning of Kingston"; "*Phoenix* and the *Rose*"; "*Old Ben Franklin* and the *Sloop Sally B.*"; "Moon in the Pear Tree"; "Erie Canal"; "Yankee Doodle"; "This Is a Land"; "Big Bill Snyder"; "Hudson Whalers"; "Follow the Drinkin' Gourd"; "Hudson River Steamboat"; "Knickerbocker Line"; and "Of Time and Rivers Flowing."

North Carolina

322. Brown, Frank C. *Folk Ballads from North Carolina* and *Folk Songs from North Carolina*. Durham, NC: Duke University Press, 1952.

323. Henry, Mellinger E., and Maurice Matteson. *Twenty-Nine Beech Mountain Folk Songs and Ballads*. New York: G. Schirmer, 1936.

324. Scarborough, Dorothy. *A Song Catcher in Southern Mountains: American Folk Songs of British Ancestry*. New York: Columbia University Press, 1937.

325. Warner, Anne. *Traditional American Folk Songs from the Anne and Frank Warner Collection*. Syracuse, NY: Syracuse University Press, 1984.

326. *North Carolina Ballads*. Performed by Artus Moser. Smithsonian/Folkways 02112, Washington, DC, 1956. audiocassette and compact disc.

    Descriptive notes and lyrics are included with this recording, which features titles such as: "Sourwood Mountain"; "Swannoanoa Town"; "Old Man over the Hill"; "Old Grey Mare"; "Two Sisters"; "Wildwood Flower"; "False Knight upon the Road"; "Cumberland Gap"; "Lord Randall"; "Poor Ellen Smith"; and "Sweet Rivers."

Ohio

327. Eddy, Mary O. *Ballads and Songs from Ohio*. New York: J. J. Augustin, 1939.

328. *Ohio State Ballads*. Performed by Anne Grimes. Smithsonian/Folkways 05217, Washington, DC, 1957. audiocassette and compact disc.
    Descriptive notes and lyrics are provided with this recording. Titles include: "Pleasant Ohio"; "Battle of Point Pleasant"; "Logan's Lament"; "Lass of Loch Royal"; "St. Clair's Defeat"; "Portsmouth Fellows"; "Christ in the Garden"; "Farmer's Curst Wife"; "Girls of Ohio"; "Alphabet Song"; "Darling Nellie Gray"; "Underground Railroad"; "My Station's Gonna Be Changed"; "O Ho! The Copperheads"; "Dying Volunteer"; "Ohio Guards"; "Ohio River Blues"; "Up on the Housetops"; and "Old Dan Tucker."

Pennsylvania

329. Korson, George. *Minstrels of the Mine Patch*. 1938. Reprint, Hatboro, PA: Folklore Associates, 1964.

330. ———. *Pennsylvania Songs and Legends*. Philadelphia: University of Pennsylvania Press, 1943. Reprint, Hatboro, PA: Folklore Associates, 1965.

331. Shoemaker, Henry. *Mountain Minstrelsy of Pennsylvania*. Philadelphia: Newman F. McGirr, 1931.

South Carolina

332. Joiner, Charles. *Folk Song in South Carolina*. Columbia, SC: University of South Carolina Press, 1971. [P]

Tennessee

333. Burton, Thomas G., and Ambrose N. Manning. *East Tennessee State University Collection of Folklore: Folksongs*. vols. I and II. Johnson City, TN: East Tennessee State University, 1967, 1969.

Utah

334. Cheyney, Thomas. *Mormon Songs from the Rocky Mountains.* 1968. Reprint, Salt Lake City, UT: University of Utah Press, 1981.

335. Hubbard, Lester A. *Ballads and Songs from Utah.* Salt Lake City, UT: University of Utah Press, 1961.

336. *Folk Songs of Idaho and Utah.* Performed by Rosalie Sorrels. Smithsonian/Folksways 05343, Washington, DC, 1961. audiocassette and compact disc.
    This recording provides descriptive notes and lyrics for the following songs: "Lynman's Hymn"; "Brigham Young"; "Winter Song"; "Death of Kathy Fiscus"; "I'll Give You My Story"; "The Girl That Played Injun with Me"; "Utah's Dixie"; "Empty Cots in the Bunkhouse Tonight"; "Tying Knots in the Devil's Tail"; "The Fox"; "Way Out in Idaho"; "My Last Cigar"; "Wreck of Old Number Nine"; "House Carpenter"; "Wild Colonial Boy"; "I Left My Baby"; and "Philadelphia Lawyer."

Vermont

337. Flanders, Helen Harkness, and George Brown. *Vermont Folksongs and Ballads.* 1931. Reprint, Detroit, MI: Gale Research, 1970.

338. Flanders, Helen Harkness, George Brown, and Phillips Barry. *The New Green Mountain Songster.* New Haven, CT: Yale University Press, 1939.

339. Sturgis, Edith B., and Robert Hughes. *Songs from the Hills of Vermont.* New York: G. Schirmer, 1919.

340. *Folksongs of Vermont.* Performed by Margaret MacArthur. Smithsonian/Folkways 05314, Washington, DC, 1963. audiocassette and compact disc.
    Descriptive notes and lyrics are provided with this recording which includes titles such as: "Needle's Eye"; "Carrion Crow"; "Gypsy Davy"; "Jenny Jenkins"; "Linktum Blue"; "Cherries Are Ripe"; "Trot, Trot to Boston"; "This Very Unhappy Man"; "Aunt Jemima"; "Gorion-Og"; "Scolding Wife"; "Riddles"; "Old Mr. Grumble"; "Single Again"; "New Hampshire Miller"; "What the Old Hen Said"; "Mother in the Graveyard"; and "Marlboro Merchants."

Virginia

341. Davis, Arthur Kyle Jr. *Folk-Songs of Virginia*. Durham, NC: Duke University Press, 1949.

342. ———. *More Traditional Ballads of Virginia*. Cambridge, MA: Harvard University Press, 1929.

343. Scarborough, Dorothy. *A Song Catcher in Southern Mountains: American Folk Songs of British Ancestry*. New York: Columbia University Press, 1937.

344. *Folksongs and Ballads of Virginia*. Performed by Paul Clayton. Smithsonian/Folkways 04703, Washington, DC, 1956. audiocassette and compact disc.
    This recording provides descriptive notes and lyrics. Titles include: "Railroad Bill"; "In the Pines"; "Gambling Man"; "Wild Rover"; "Bill Dooley"; "Talt Hall"; "Farmer's Curst Wife"; "Harvey Logan"; "Lady Margaret"; "Frankie"; "If I Had a Bottle of Rum"; "Lord Darnell"; "Poor Little Maids"; and "Little Pig."

West Virginia

345. Boette, Marie. *Singa Hipsy Doodle and Other Folk Songs of West Virginia*. Parsons, WV: McClain Printing, 1971.

346. Bush, Michael E. *Folk Songs of Central West Virginia*. Ravenswood, WV: Custom Printing, 1969.

347. Cox, John Harrington. *Folksongs Mainly from West Virginia*. 1964. Reprint, New York: Da Capo Press, 1977. [P]

348. Gainer, Patrick. *Folk Songs from the West Virginia Hills*. Grantsville, WV: Seneca Books, 1975.

Wisconsin

349. Peters, Harry B. *Folk Songs Out of Wisconsin*. Madison, WI: State Historical Society of Wisconsin, 1977.

Transportation

General

 Book

350. Reid, Rob. *Children's Jukebox: A Subject Guide to Musical Recordings and Programming Ideas for Songsters Ages 1 to 12*. Chicago: American Library Association, 1995. 225pp.

   Arranged by subject, this select guide provides the titles for contemporary children's songs along with the performing artist, title of recording, publication date, and distributor. Titles are listed alphabetically within each subject, and a brief annotation describes the song and often includes programming ideas. See section titled "Transportation." A good index is provided.

 Recording

351. *Transportation*. Twin Sisters Productions, 1995. (1340 Home Ave., Akron, OH 44310) audiocassette, 45 min. Grades K–2.

   Old and new songs are presented about all kinds of transportation—planes, trains, trucks, buses, balloons, bikes, cars, bulldozers, and space shuttles. A 24-page booklet with lyrics and reproducible activity sheets is included.

Canalboats

(*See also* States: Ohio, New York)

 Books

352. Hullfish, William. *The Canaller's Songbook*. York, PA: American Canal and Transportation Center, 1984. (809 Rathton Road, York, PA 17403) 87pp. Arr. for guitar. [P]

   This is a collection of 37 songs, some sung by canallers on the Erie and other canals, and others sung by entertainers of the day in minstrel and vaudeville shows. A bibliography is included. Accompanying audiocassette and compact disc recorded by the Golden Eagle String Band are available from Audio Image Studio, Hilton, New York.

353. Silverman, Jerry. *Songs of the Sea, Rivers, Lakes and Canals*. Pacific, MO: Mel Bay Publications, 1992. 208pp. Arr. for piano and guitar. [P]

This is a collection of 106 songs, with brief notes, some of which relate to the Erie Canal.

 Recordings

354. *Grand Canal Ballads: Songs of the Erie Canal*. Performed by the Golden Eagle String Band. Folkways/Smithsonian 32318, Washington, DC, 1981. audiocassette and compact disc.

Descriptive notes and lyrics are provided with this recording, which includes these titles: "Oh! Dat Low Bridge"; "Paddy on the Canal"; "Dark-Eyed Canaller"; "I'm Afloat on the Erie Canal"; "Ballad of the Erie Canal"; "Boating on a Bull-Head"; "Meeting on the Waters of the Hudson and the Erie"; "The Er-i-e"; "A Trip on the Erie"; "That Long Canal"; "Canawler, Canawler—Hogee on the Towpath"; "The Raging Canal"; "The Aged Pilot Man"; and "Low Bridge, Everybody Down."

355. *Oh! That Low Bridge: Songs of the Erie Canal*. Performed by George Ward. Front Hall Records, FHR-028. (RD1, Drawer A, Voorheesville, NY 12186)

Songs include: "Paddy on the Canal"; "The Meeting of the Waters"; "Michigan-I-Ay"; "I'm Afloat!"; "Attend All Ye Drivers"; and "The Girl from Yewdall's Mill."

Railroad

(*See also* American History: Westward Expansion; Regions: West)

 Pamphlets

356. *Scott, John Anthony, and Laurence I. Seidman. "Railroads: Their History, People and Songs," *Folksong in the Classroom* VI, no. 1 (fall 1986): 1–24. (P.O. Box 925, Sturbridge, MA 01566) Arr. for guitar. Grades 4+.

This provides a good introduction to the history, heroes, and songs of the railroad. Titles include: "Casey Jones"; "Five Hundred Miles"; "John Henry"; "Nine Hundred Miles"; "Paddy Works on the Railroad"; "A Railroader for Me"; "This Train"; "Track Laying Song"; "Wabash Cannonball"; and "The Workingman's Train." This resource also includes additional teaching ideas for follow-up activities. A bibliography and discography are provided.

90 / SOCIAL STUDIES

357. Silverman, Jerry. *Train Songs*. Pacific, MO: Mel Bay, 1991. 151pp. Arr. for piano. [P]

　　Silverman, a compiler of folksong collections, has put together 73 songs and one poem about railroads, railroading, and railroaders.

 Recordings

358. Cash, Johnny. *Ridin' the Rail: The Great American Train Story*. Sony Video Software, 1983. videocassette, 52 min.

　　Johnny Cash hosts this program that traces the history of trains and railroads in the United States. Included are many period folksongs and popular songs about trains, railroad workers, and more.

359. *Western Railroad Songs*. Performed by Keith McNeil and Rusty McNeil. WEM Records, 1994. (16230 Van Buren Blvd., Riverside, CA 92504) 2 audiocassettes, 180 min. Grades 5+.

　　These songs and narration explore the historical, political, social, and economic events connected with the western railroads of the nineteenth and twentieth century, including sections on builders, railroaders, and transcontinental trains. Titles include: "900 Miles"; "A Railroader for Me"; "Railroad Traveler"; "Rock Island Line"; "Great Rock Island Route"; "Kansas Land"; "Subsidy, a Goat Island Ballad"; "John Chinaman, My Jo"; "Twelve Hundred More"; "Mick upon the Railroad"; "Tamping Ties"; "Drill Ye Terriers"; "The Iron Horse"; "Hell-Bound Train"; "Chinese Breakdown"; "Gamblin' Blackie"; "The Regular Army, Oh"; "Handcart Song"; "Echo Canyon"; "Railroading on the Great Divide"; "Pullman Porters on Parade"; "Zack, the Mormon Engineer"; "Roving Gambler"; "Jesse James"; "Life's Railway to Heaven"; "Railroad Boomer"; "There's Many a Man Killed on the Railroad"; "Only a Brakeman"; "Little Red Caboose Behind the Train"; "Asleep at the Switch"; "Please Mister Conductor"; "Dying Hogger"; "Danville Girl"; "Wabash Cannonball"; "Big Rock Candy Mountain"; "Bum Song"; "Hallelujah I'm a Bum"; "In the Baggage Coach Ahead"; "Harvey Girls"; "Way Out in Idaho"; "Immigration Song"; "Peninsula Pike"; "Mike"; "Casey Jones"; "Rosenthal's Goat"; "Old Jay Gould"; "Oh Jimmy Fisk, My Jo Jim"; and "Jim Fisk."

 Further Reading

360. Carpenter, Ann Miller. "The Railroad in American Folksong, 1865–1920," in *Diamond Bessie and The Sheperds*, edited by Wilson M. Hudson, 103–19. Austin, TX: Encino Press, 1972.

361. Cohen, Norm. *Long Steel Rail: The Railroad in American Folksong*. Urbana, IL: University of Illinois Press, 1981. 710pp.

This is a detailed, scholarly study of railroads with a brief history of the railroad in America and an in-depth discussion of specific railroad songs, including the following categories: heroes and badmen, disasters, hoboes, blues, and work. A bibliography and discography are included.

Riverboats

(*See also* States: Ohio, Mississippi)

 Pamphlets

362. Scott, John A., and Laurence I. Seidman. "Rivers of America, Part I & II," *Folksong in the Classroom* VII, no. 2 and 3 (winter/spring 1987): 1–42. (P.O. Box 925, Sturbridge, MA 01566) Arr. for guitar. Grades 4+. [ED 344784]

The authors, both longtime teachers with extensive experience using folksong to teach social studies and the humanities, offer a means for studying rivers.

Part I provides information and background material on using folksongs to examine American rivers in the context of economic life, transportation, national identity, exploration, settlement and urbanization, politics, and Native Americans. Titles include: "One More River"; A La Claire Fontaine"; "Hudson River Steamboat"; "Banks of the Sacramento"; "Red River Valley"; "Banks of the Ohio"; "Coffee Grows on White Oak Trees"; "All Quiet on the Potomac"; and "No More Cane on the Brazos."

Part II explores issues related to ecology, natural resources, wildlife and science, literature, folklore and the arts, and the dimensions of human tragedy in the struggle and use of rivers. The following titles are provided: "My Bark Canoe"; "Death of General Wolfe"; "Ballad of Peter Gray"; "Lovely Ohio"; "Way Down Yonder in the Paw Paw Patch"; "We're Coming Arkansas"; "Down by the Riverside"; "Roll on Columbia"; and "My Dirty Stream." Follow-up activities and a bibliography are also provided.

363. Silverman, Jerry. *Songs of the Sea, Rivers, Lakes and Canals.* Pacific, MO: Mel Bay, 1992. 208pp. Arr. for piano and guitar. [P]

Silverman, a prolific compiler of folksong collections, has put together a songbook of 106 songs along with brief notes. A number of the songs deal with sailors' work and lives and with famous ships.

Further Sources of Songs

364. Wheeler, Mary. *Steamboatin' Days: Folk Songs of the River Packet Era.* 1944. Reprint, Salem, NH: Ayer Company, 1977. 121pp.
   This collection contains 66 songs, primarily from African American workers on the Ohio and Mississippi rivers.

Ships

(See also Occupations: Sailors, Whalers)

 Book

365. Silverman, Jerry. *Songs of the Sea, Rivers, Lakes and Canals.* Pacific, MO: Mel Bay, 1992. 208pp. Arr. for piano and guitar. [P]
   Among the 106 songs in this collection are a number of songs used for work and recreation aboard deep-water sailing vessels.

 Pamphlets

366. Kracht, James B. "Worth Ten Men on a Rope." Galveston, TX: National Marine Education Association, 1981: 11. Grades 5+.
   Songs served an important purpose on the old sailing ships because they often provided a rhythm to which the sailors could work in unison; hence the old saying that a shanty (work song) was worth "ten men on a rope." This is a lesson guide on sea shanties, with lyrics to these four: "Paddy Doyle"; "Haul Away Joe"; "Leave Her, Johnny"; and "Fire! Fire!"

367. *Scott, John Anthony, and Laurence I. Seidman. "Songs of the Sea: Chanties, Fo'c'sle and Fishing Songs," *Folksong in the Classroom* IV, no. 2 (winter 1984): 31–52. (P.O. Box 925, Sturbridge, MA 01566) Arr. for guitar. [P] Grades 4+. [ED 273507]
   In this work the authors explain the importance of shanties and other songs at sea for work and fo'c'sle (forecastle, or entertainment). Extensive background notes, plus follow-up ideas are given for the following songs: "Boney"; "Haul Away Joe"; "Lowlands"; "Blood Red Roses"; "Shenandoah"; "Bound for the Rio Grande"; "Henry Martin"; "Banks of Newfoundland"; "Lord Franklin"; "Boston Come All Ye"; and "A Trip to the Grand Banks." A bibliography is included.

Recordings

368. *Fo'c'sle Songs and Shanties.* Performed by Paul Clayton and the Fo'c'sle Singers. Smithsonian/Folkways 02429, Washington, DC, 1959. audiocassette and compact disc.
  Descriptive notes and lyrics are provided with this recording, which includes such titles as: "Ratcliffe Highway"; "Rio Grande"; "Haul on the Bowline"; "Maggie May"; "Leave Her Johnny"; "Paddy Lay Back"; "Fire Down Below"; "A Hundred Years Ago"; "Santy Anno"; "Captain Nipper"; "Hanging Johnny"; "Banks of Sacramento"; and "Won't You Go My Way."

369. **Roll and Go, The Shantyman's Day Aboard a Yankee Clipper.* Performed by Bill Bonyun. Heirloom Records 504. (Route 2, Wiscasset, ME 04518) audiocassette.
  Tells about a day in the life of a shantyman through both narrative and song. A teacher's guide is provided. See entry 246.

 Further Sources of Songs

370. Colcord, Joanna. *Songs of American Sailormen.* 1924. Reprint, New York: W. W. Norton, 1937. 212pp. (Originally published as *Roll and Go, Songs of American Sailormen*)
  This is a good collection of 109 sailor songs, which includes useful commentary.

371. Hugill, Stan. *Shanties from the Seven Seas.* 1961. Reprint, Mystic, CT: Mystic Seaport Museum, 1994. 609pp.
  Hugill, an authority on sailor songs, actually served as a shantyman. This comprehensive collection of several hundred shanties is considered the best source on the subject of sea shanties.

Women's History
(*See also* American History: Post-World War II;
Occupations: Miners, Mill Workers)

 Book

372. Wenner, Hilda E., and Elizabeth Freilicher. *Here's to the Women: 100 Songs for and About American Women.* Syracuse, NY: Syracuse University Press, 1987. 350pp. Arr. for guitar.
  This collection contains contemporary songs as well as traditional and historical songs that deal with labor and social movements in American history. A bibliography and discography are included.

🎵 Pamphlet

373. Scott, John Anthony, and Laurence I. Seidman. "Women's Songs," *Folksong in the Classroom* IV, no. 1 (autumn 1983): 8–21. (P.O. Box 925, Sturbridge, MA 01566) Arr. for guitar. Grades 5+.

    A humanities resource that devotes each issue to a specific topic, this issue covers songs about women. Songs, grouped by topic, include: (Women and Warriors) "The Bonnie Lass of Fyvie"; "Mrs. McGraw"; (The Frontier Experience) "The Wisconsin Emigrant"; "The Single Girl"; "The Lullaby: Deirin Dé"; (Women's Laments) "Dewy Dens of Yarrow"; "All My Trials"; (Marriage) "The Trees They Do Grow High"; (Love Songs) "Come All Ye Fair and Tender Ladies"; "Must I Be Bound?"; "I Never Will Marry"; (Worker and Mother) "The Mill Mother's Lament"; "The Housewife's Lament"; and (Women and the Vote) "Keep Women in Their Place." This resource also includes suggested follow-up activities for classroom use as well as a bibliography.

🎵 Recording

374. *Songs of the Suffragettes*. Performed by Elizabeth Knight. Smithsonian/Folkways 50281, Washington, DC, 1958. audiocassette and compact disc.

    Descriptive notes and lyrics are provided with this recording, which includes such titles as: "Columbia's Daughters"; "Uncle Sam's Wedding"; "Keep Woman in Her Sphere"; "Let Us All Speak Our Minds"; "Taxation Tyranny"; "Promised Land"; "Suffrage Flag"; "Winning the Vote"; "Give the Ballot to the Mothers"; "Song of Wyoming"; "Going to the Polls"; "Where Are the Boys Today?"; "Yellow Ribbon"; "Hallelujah"; "Oh, Dear, What Can the Matter Be?"; and "New America."

World Cultures
(*See also* American History: Immigration)

General

375. *For a catalog of excellent multicultural music books, recordings, videos, and choral music for educators, write to World Music Press, P.O. Box 2565, Danbury, CT 06813.

376. *For an excellent, extensive bibliography on specific countries and regions of the world, see Judith Cook Tucker, "Circling the Globe: Multiultural Resources," *Music Educators Journal* (May 1992): 37–42.

Article

377. Anderson, William M. "Cultural Consciousness in Teaching General Music," *Music Educators Journal* (May 1992): 30–36.
      Anderson provides a rational approach for integrating multicultural activities into music education and provides lesson plans (with text and melody) for use of a specific song from the Native American, African American, and Filipino traditions.

 Books

378. *Campbell, Patricia Shehan. *Traditional Songs of Singing Cultures: A World Sampler*. Miami, FL: Warner Bros. Publications, 1996. 64pp. Accompanying compact disc. Grades 3+.
      This is a collection of folksongs, with activities, cultural information, and maps for 20 different cultures.

379. *Campbell, Patricia Shehan, Ellen McCullough-Brabson, and Judith Cook Tucker. *Roots and Branches: A Legacy of Multicultural Music for Children*. Danbury, CT: World Music Press, 1994. [P] Grades 1–6.
      This textbook includes a recording (audiocassette or compact disc) and presents a collection of 38 songs from 23 cultures from Africa, Asia, the Caribbean, Europe, the Middle East, North America, and South America. The set includes stories, descriptions of each culture, and songs in the original languages with accompanying translations and pronunciation guide. A bibliography and maps are provided.

380. *Jessup, Lynne. *World Music: A Source Book for Teaching*. Danbury, CT: World Music Press, 1988. 64pp. [P]
      This annotated resource guide to books, recordings, and films deals with musical traditions of a wide variety of cultures and is suitable for all grades. It includes addresses for manufacturers and distributors.

381. *Tooze, Ruth, and Beatrice Perham Krone. *Literature and Music As Resources for Social Studies*. Englewood Cliffs, NJ: Prentice-Hall, 1955. 457pp.
      Although the children's book selections are dated, this is a marvelous source of ideas for combining children's literature with social studies. Some songs are included. See sections on Mexico, Europe, the Near East, Africa, Australia, New Zealand, and the Philippines. Bibliographies are provided.

Recordings

382. For cassettes and compact discs of authentic performances of folk music from around the world, the largest single source is Smithsonian/Folkways Recordings, Center for Folklife Programs, 955 L'Enfant Plaza, Suite 2600, MRC 914, Washington, DC 20560. Write for the catalog.

383. *Ella Jenkins: Multi-cultural Children's Songs. Smithsonian/Folkways 45045, Washington, DC, 1995. audiocassette and compact disc, 69 min. Grades 1–4.

Descriptive notes and lyrics, plus activities for 23 traditional and contemporary songs and chants from Africa, New Zealand, Poland, Syria, America, and more are presented with this recording. Titles include: "The World Is Big, the World Is Small"; "Hello"; "Greetings in Many Languages"; "Jambo"; "Tahboo"; "On Safari"; "Counting in Swahili"; "Mexican Handclapping Song"; "Dulce, Dulce"; "In Trinidad"; "Caney Mi Macaro"; "Yodeling Song"; "Dredle, Dredle, Dredle"; "Rabbi Teaches ABC's"; "English ABC"; "Greeting in Arabic"; "Balloon Song"; "Maori Chant"; "Play Your Instruments"; "May-Ree Mack"; "We Are Native American Tribes"; "A Neighborhood Is a Friendly Place"; and "Thank You in Many Languages."

384. *The JVC Video Anthology of World Music and Dance*. Victor Company of Japan, 1991. (Available through Smithsonian/Folkways Records) videocassettes, 57–59 min. each. Grades 7+.

This collection of 30 videotapes contains examples of music and dance from eight major regions of the world and provides eight accompanying guides written by area specialists. Guide One is an introduction to the entire series.

Series Titles include:
1. *The JVC Video Anthology of World Music and Dance, vol. 1: East Asia I, Korea 1*
2. *The JVC Video Anthology of World Music and Dance, vol. 2: East Asia II, Korea 2*
3. *The JVC Video Anthology of World Music and Dance, vol. 3: East Asia III, China 1*
4. *The JVC Video Anthology of World Music and Dance, vol. 4: East Asia IV, China 2*
5. *The JVC Video Anthology of World Music and Dance, vol. 5: East Asia V, China 3, Mongolia*
6. *The JVC Video Anthology of World Music and Dance, vol. 6: Southeast Asia I, Vietnam, Cambodia*
7. *The JVC Video Anthology of World Music and Dance, vol. 7: Southeast Asia II, Thailand, Burma*
8. *The JVC Video Anthology of World Music and Dance, vol. 8: Southeast Asia III, Malaysia, Philippines*

9. *The JVC Video Anthology of World Music and Dance, vol. 9: Southeast Asia IV, Indonesia 1*
10. *The JVC Video Anthology of World Music and Dance, vol. 10: Southeast Asia V, Indonesia 2*
11. *The JVC Video Anthology of World Music and Dance, vol. 11: South Asia I, India 1*
12. *The JVC Video Anthology of World Music and Dance, vol. 12: South Asia II, India 2*
13. *The JVC Video Anthology of World Music and Dance, vol. 13: South Asia III, India 3*
14. *The JVC Video Anthology of World Music and Dance, vol. 14: South Asia IV, Pakistan, Bangladesh*
15. *The JVC Video Anthology of World Music and Dance, vol. 15: South Asia V, Sri Lanka, Nepal, Bhutan*
16. *The JVC Video Anthology of World Music and Dance, vol. 16: Middle East and Africa I, Turkey, Iran, Iraq, Lebanon, Qatar*
17. *The JVC Video Anthology of World Music and Dance, vol. 17: Middle East and Africa II, Egypt, Tunisia, Morocco, Mali, Cameroon, Zaire, Tunisia*
18. *The JVC Video Anthology of World Music and Dance, vol. 18: Middle East III, Chad, Cameroon*
19. *The JVC Video Anthology of World Music and Dance, vol. 19: Middle East IV, Ivory Coast, Botswana, Republic of South Africa*
20. *The JVC Video Anthology of World Music and Dance, vol. 20: Europe I, Ireland, England, France, Switzerland, West Germany, Spain, Italy, Greece*
21. *The JVC Video Anthology of World Music and Dance, vol. 21: Europe II, Poland, Czechoslovakia, Hungary*
22. *The JVC Video Anthology of World Music and Dance, vol. 22: Europe III, Romania, Yugoslavia, Bulgaria, Albania*
23. *The JVC Video Anthology of World Music and Dance, vol. 23: Soviet Union I, Russia*
24. *The JVC Video Anthology of World Music and Dance, vol. 24: Soviet Union II, Latvia, Estonia, Lithuania, Belorussia, Ukraine, Moldavia*
25. *The JVC Video Anthology of World Music and Dance, vol. 25: Soviet Union III, Azerbaijan, Armenia, Georgia, Dagestan*
26. *The JVC Video Anthology of World Music and Dance, vol. 26: Soviet Union IV, Kazakh, Uzbek, Turkmen, Tajik, Kirgiz, Kalmyk, Mari, Bashkir, Siberia*
27. *The JVC Video Anthology of World Music and Dance, vol. 27: The Americas I, North American Indians*

28. *The JVC Video Anthology of World Music and Dance*, vol. 28: *The Americas II, Mexico, Cuba, Bolivia, Argentina*
29. *The JVC Video Anthology of World Music and Dance*, vol. 29: *Oceania I, Micronesia, Melanesia*
30. *The JVC Video Anthology of World Music and Dance*, vol. 30: *Oceania II Polynesia, New Zealand*

385. Sounds of the World series. Reston, VA: Music Educators National Conference. audiocassette. Grades 5+.
    This collection is comprised of three audiotapes that include performances, interviews, descriptions of cultural context, and a teaching guide with lessons on the music of the Caribbean, Southeast Asia, Middle East, Mexico, East Europe, China, and Japan for music, social science, and humanities classes.

386. *Where I Come From! Songs and Poems from Many Cultures*. By Victor Cockburn and Judith Steinbergh. Talking Stone Press, Chestnut Hill, VA, 1992. (99 Evans Road, Brookline, MA 02146) 2 audiocassettes, 120 min. each. Grades 5+.
    Cockburn, an experienced school performing artist, has put together a collection of 63 traditional and contemporary songs, poems, and chants from different cultures and countries, performed in a variety of languages (English, Chinese, Japanese, Arabic, French, Hawaiian, Gaelic, Hebrew, Russian, Spanish, and Vietnamese). A number of songs were written by students. Categories include home and community, family and culture, using your senses, inspiration, and seasons and nature. A 24-page teacher's guide with activities and lyrics is provided.

 Further Sources of Songs

387. Heywood, Charles. *Folk Songs of the World*. New York: John Day, 1966. Arr. for guitar.
    More than 100 countries from around the world are represented in this collection of 180 songs. Good introductory comments on the musical cultures of each area and context notes with the original language and English translation are provided for each song.

 Further Reading

388. May, Elizabeth, ed. *Musics of Many Cultures: An Introduction*. Los Angeles: University of California Press, 1980. [P]
    This is a good collection of essays on world music by experts in the field. Articles are included on African, Asian, Native American,

Indonesian, Middle Eastern, and South American music. Bibliographies and annotated film lists are provided.

Africa

(*See also* African Americans; World Cultures: General)

 Articles

389. Hopton-Jones, Pamela. "Introducing the Music of East Africa," *Music Educators Journal* 82 (November 1995): 26–30.
    This is an interview with an ethnomusicologist that explores the cultural and historical context of East African songs and music. There is also a lesson plan for the teaching of a song and a select list of resources.

390. *Lindquist, Barbara Reeder. "Sub-Saharan Africa," in *Multicultural Perspectives in Music Education*, edited by William M. Anderson and Patricia Shehan Campbell, 145–79. Reston, VA: Music Educators National Conference, 1989. Grades 7+.
    This article provides commentary on the characteristics of African music as well as six lesson plans. Topics covered are: polyrhythms and use of marimbas; tonal language; exposure to recorded performances; and lessons in ensembling a selection from Zimbabwe called "Maiwe," for teaching two songs from Ghana, and for recognizing musical examples from West, East, and South Africa. A bibliography, discography, filmography, and maps are provided.

 Book

391. *Standifer, James A., and Barbara Reeder Lindquist. *Source Book of African and Afro-American Materials for Music Educators*. Reston, VA: Music Educators National Conference, 1972.
    This is an excellent collection of resources that includes bibliographies, filmographies, and information on musicians and music styles.

 Recording

392. *The JVC/Smithsonian Folkways Video Anthology of Music and Dance of Africa*. 3 vols. Smithsonian/Folkways C 4506-4508, Washington, DC, c.1996.

Asia

(*See also* World Cultures: General, India)

 *Articles*

393. Campbell, Patricia Shehan. "Bell Yung on Music of China," *Music Educators Journal* 81 (September 24, 1994): 39–46.

    This is an interview with an ethnomusicologist who discusses the cultural and historical context of Chinese songs and music making. Lesson plans are included for teaching the song "Chinese Festival Music" and the music piece "Chinese Instrumental Music." A discography is provided.

394. Campbell, Patricia Shehan, and William M. Anderson. "Southeast Asia," in *Multicultural Perspectives in Music Education*, 281–94. Reston, VA: Music Educators National Conference, 1989. Grades 4+.

    This article discusses the characteristics of the music of Cambodia, Laos, Thailand, Vietnam, and Indonesia. Four lesson plans are provided on songs and instruments. The first lesson aims at familiarizing students with the music and culture of the region; the second exposes students to the instruments of the *pi phat* orchestra; the third introduces students to the national instrument of Laos, the *kaen*; and the fourth teaches the Thai birthday song "Phleng Wan Koet." A bibliography, discography, and filmography are included.

395. *Kuo-Huang, Han, Ricardo Trimillos, and William M. Anderson. "East Asia," in *Multicultural Perspectives in Music Education*, edited by William M. Anderson and Patricia Shehan Campbell, 239–80. Reston, VA: Music Educators National Conference, 1989. Grades 6+.

    This article provides a good overview of the history and music of Japan and China by three ethnomusicologists. Five lesson plans on music in Chinese culture are included. Lesson one presents two Chinese songs, "The Eldest Daughter of the Jiang Family" and "Jasmine Flowers of the Sixth Moon" and examines the pentatonic scale. Lesson two describes a Chinese percussion ensemble. Lesson three presents the song "Fuhng Yang Wa Gu" (Flower Drum Song), which combines knowledge of the pentatonic scale and percussion. Lesson four introduces students to the instruments *zheng* and *xiao*. Lesson five examines Chinese opera. These topics are also included: the instruments of a Japanese *gagaku* orchestra; variations of a song; Japanese *noh* theatre *kabuki* theatre; and the instrument *shakuhachi*. A bibliography and discography are provided.

396. *"Teaching the Music of Asian Americans," in *Teaching Music with a Multicultural Approach*, edited by William M. Anderson, 49–64. Reston, VA: Music Educators National Conference, 1991.

  This article describes Chinese music traditions and provides a lesson plan for the use of two songs, "The Flower Drum" and "The Eldest Daughter of the Jiang Family." A bibliography and discography are included.

♪ Recordings

397. *Discovering the Music of Japan*. AMS Media. (9710 DeSoto Ave., Chatsworth, CA 41311-4409) videocassette, 21 min., color. Grades 3–6.

  This video takes the viewer to a Japanese teahouse where three major instruments, the *koto*, the *shakuhaci*, and the *shamisen* are demonstrated and are used to accompany a number of traditional songs and dances. A brief, but useful, lesson guide is also included.

398. *Music of East Asia: Chinese, Korean and Japanese*. Sounds of the World series. Music Educators National Conference, Reston, VA, 1989. 3 audiocassettes. Grades 5+.

  This resource is comprised of three tapes that include performances of refugees now living in the United States. A teacher's guide with transcriptions for some of the music is provided as well.

399. *Music of Southeast Asia: Lao, Hmong, and Vietnamese*. Sounds of the World series. Music Educators National Conference, Reston, VA, 1986. 3 audiocassettes.

  This resource comprises three tapes that include performances of refugees now living in the United States as well as a teacher's guide with transcriptions for some of the music.

400. *Teaching the Music of Asian Americans*. Music Educators National Conference, Reston, VA, c. 1991. videocassette, 36 min.

  Ethnomusicologist Kuo-Huang Han presents an overview of the music and culture of China from the Zhou dynasty to the present day and includes instruction on how to teach it. Demonstrations of Chinese opera, folksongs, simple chants, and instruments are provided as well as a teacher's guide.

Further Reading

401. Liang, Minguye. *Music of the Billion: An Introduction to Chinese Music Culture*. New York: Heinrichshofen Edition, 1985.

  This is probably the best and most comprehensive book available on Chinese music in English, with useful general descriptions of musical instruments and many musical examples. A discography is included.

Canada

 Article

402. Dhand, Harry. "Musical Reflections of Canada's History," *Social Education* 35, no. 6 (1971): 624–27. Grades 4+.
    This article features 11 songs that highlight events, people, and customs from Canadian history. A list of songs and records that further illustrate eras in Canada's history is also provided. A bibliography is included.

 Book

403. *Fowke, Edith, and Alan Mills. *Singing Our History: Canada's Story in Song*, 1965. Reprint, Toronto: Doubleday Canada, 1984. 249pp. Arr. for piano. (Original title: *Canada's Story in Song*)
    In this book two of Canada's best-known folklorists provide context and background for 75 songs through which the story of Canada can be told from pre-European times to the late nineteenth century. A bibliography and discography are included.

 Pamphlet

404. Scott, John Anthony, John W. Scott, and Laurence Seidman. "Songs of Newfoundland," *Folksong in the Classroom* XI, no. 1 (fall 1990): 4–26. (P.O. Box 925, Sturbridge, MA 01566) Arr. for guitar. [P] Grades 5+. [ED 340627]
    This resource examines Newfoundland's people, history, and culture through its folksongs. Along with a short but good introduction, the following nine songs are given: "Bonny Banks of Virgie"; "Isabeau S'y Promene" (French and English versions); "Brave Wolfe"; "Sailor's Alphabet"; "The Banks of Newfoundland"; "Dark-Eyed Sailor"; "She's Like the Swallow"; and "Loss of the *Danny Goodwin*." A bibliography, discography, and index of Newfoundland songs from previous issues are provided.

 Recordings

405. *JVC/Smithsonian Folkways Video Anthology of Music and Dance of the Americas, vol. 1: Canada and the United States*. Multicultural Media, Montpelier, VT, 1995. videocassette, 60 min., color. Grades 5+.
    The first side of this video features performances of instrumental, vocal, and dance music from French-speaking and English-speaking communities in Canada. A 78-page booklet provides an overview essay, selection descriptions, a list of resource material, and suggested activities.

406. *O Canada: A History of Canada in Song*. Performed by Alan Mills. Smithsonian/Folkways 03001, Washington, DC. audiocassette and compact disc.
    Descriptive notes and lyrics to folksongs and historical songs that trace the history of Canada are presented here. Titles include: "Eskimo Weather Chant"; "Iroquois Lullaby"; "A Saint-Malo"; "Vive les Matelots!"; "A La Claire Fontaine"; "*Golden Vanity*"; "Huron Christmas Carol"; "En Roulant Ma Boule"; "Petit Rocher"; "Tenaouich' Tenaga"; "Ballad of New Scotland"; "La Courte Paille"; "Brave Wolfe"; "General Wolfe"; "Revolutionary Tea"; "Marching down to Old Quebec"; "Le Sergent"; "Come All Ye Bold Canadians"; "Battle of Queenstown Heights"; "*Chesapeake* and the *Shannon*"; "*Sir Robert Peel*"; "Battle of the Windmill"; "Un Canadien Errant"; "Fenian Song"; "Anti-Confederation Song"; "Anti-Fenian Song"; "Prince Edward Island, Adieu"; "Pork, Beans and Hard-Tack"; "Between the Forks and Carleton"; "Maple Leaf Forever"; "O Canada!"; "La Rose Blanche"; "Franklin Expedition"; "Scarborough Settler's Lament"; "Little Old Sod Shanty"; "Alberta Homesteader"; "Dying Outlaw"; "Poor Little Girls of Ontario"; "Klondike Gold Rush"; "When the Ice Worms Nest Again"; "Saskatchewan"; and "Iron Ore by 'Fifty-Four."

 Further Source of Songs

407. Fowke, Edith, and Richard Johnston. *Folk Songs of Canada*. Waterloo, Ontario: Waterloo Music, 1954. 91pp. Arr. for piano and guitar.
    This is a nice collection of 60 songs featuring Canada's history, woods, sea, plains, and more.

Europe

(*See also* World Cultures: General)

 Article

408. Campbell, Patricia Shehan. "Europe," in *Multicultural Perspectives in Music Education*, edited by William M. Anderson and Patricia Shehan Campbell, 119–44. Reston, VA: Music Educators National Conference, 1989. Arr. for guitar. Grades 4+.
    This article provides a good, although brief, coverage of various music of Europe and includes lesson plans for familiarizing students with sounds of the folk music, instruments, and dance of Ireland, France, Sweden, Spain, Bulgaria, and Hungary. Songs include: "Leaving Erin"; "Cuckoo's Egg"; and "Tygnula Bulgaria." A bibliography, discography, filmography, and map are provided.

Pamphlet

409. Rubin, Ruth, and John Anthony Scott. "The Jewish People of Eastern Europe Through Their Songs and Ballads," *Folksong in the Classroom* XIII, no. 1 (fall 1992): 5–31. (P.O. Box 925, Sturbridge, MA 01566) Arr. for guitar. [ED 391731]
> This resource gives good background and introductory notes to songs, with English translations, that deal with the Jewish experience in Eastern Europe. Titles include: "Tumbalalayka"; "Bulbes"; "Ot Azoy Nayt a Shnayder"; "Papir Iz Doch Vays"; "Oy Dortn Dortn"; "Mayn Yingele"; "Zhankoye"; "Yeder Ruft Mich Ziamele"; and "Partizaner Lid." (See also Ruth Rubin's book *Voices of a People: The Story of Yiddish Folksong*. Philadelphia, PA: Jewish Publication Society of America, 1990. This work gives a useful introduction to the history and songs of east European Jews and includes a bibliography and discography.)

 Further Sources of Songs

410. Silverman, Jerry. *Mel Bay Presents Songs of the British Isles*. Pacific, MO: Mel Bay. Arr. for guitar and piano. [P]
> This is a collection of traditional and popular songs from England, Scotland, Wales, Cornwall, and Ireland.

411. ———. *Mel Bay Presents Songs of England*. Pacific, MO: Mel Bay, c. 1991. 112pp. Arr. for guitar and piano. [P]
> Silverman delivers a pleasing collection of 100 popular folksongs from England.

412. ———. *Mel Bay Presents Songs of France*. Pacific, MO: Mel Bay, c. 1994. 83pp. Arr. for guitar and piano. [P]
> Here is a collection of 32 folksongs in French that includes English translations. The emphasis is on occupations and French history.

413. ———. *Mel Bay Presents Songs of Germany*. Pacific, MO: Mel Bay, 1996. 93pp. Arr. for guitar and piano. [P]
> This is a collection of 46 well-known German folksongs, including English translations and brief historical notes.

414. ———. *Songs of Ireland*. Pacific, MO: Mel Bay, 1991. 112pp. Arr. for guitar and piano. [P]
> This is a collection of 105 Irish and Irish American popular songs. An accompanying audiocassette is also available.

415. ———. *Mel Bay Presents Songs of Scotland*. Pacific, MO: Mel Bay, c. 1991. 111pp. Arr. for guitar and piano. [P]

Silverman provides 86 songs, including brief commentary, in three categories: traditional ballads, songs of Robert Burns, and broadsides. An accompanying audiocassette is also available.

 Recordings

416. *JVC/Smithsonian Folkways Video Anthology of Music and Dance of Europe*. 2 vols. Smithsonian/Folkways C 4504, 4505, Washington, DC, c. 1996. videocassette.

417. *Worlds of Music: East Europe: Albanian, Greek, and South Slavic*. Music Educators National Conference, Reston, VA, 1990. audiocassette.

This is a set of three tapes that include interviews with and performances by refugees now living in the United States. A teacher's guide with transcriptions for some of the music, historical background, and musical background is also provided as well as suggestions for teaching a unit on European music.

India

 Recording

418. *Discovering the Music of India*. AMS Media. (9710 DeSoto Ave., Chatsworth, CA 91311-4409) videocassette, 20 min., color. Grades 3–6.

In this video Indian musicians perform ragas on the *sitar*, flute, *tambora*, and other traditional instruments, emphasizing the importance of improvisation. A dancer demonstrates a traditional Indian dance. A brief but useful lesson guide is also included.

 Further Reading

419. Reck, David B. "India/South India," in *Worlds of Music: An Introduction to the Music of the World's Peoples*. 3d edition, edited by Jeff Todd Titon, James T. Koetting, David P. McAllester, David B. Reck, and Mark Slobin, 208–76. New York: Schirmer Books, 1992. audiocassette available. Grades 8+.

A brief but good coverage of the culture of India and a discussion of the classical music and instruments of South India are presented here, including a section on building and playing a *slide veena* and *tambura*. A bibliography and discography are included.

Latin America and the Caribbean
(*See also* World Cultures: General)

 Articles

420. Campbell, Patricia Shehan. "Anthony Seeger on Music of Amazonian Indians," *Music Educators Journal* 81, no. 4 (January 1995): 17–23.

    In this article an ethnomusicologist discusses the music of lowland Amazonian Indians, the Suya. A lesson plan for teaching songs of the seasons and ceremonies is included as well as music for the song "Why the Suya Sing."

421. ———. "Steven Loza on Latino Music," *Music Educators Journal* 82 (September 1995): 45–52.

    This is an interview with a noted ethnomusicologist who explores the cultural and historical context of songs and music-making in South America. A lesson plan is included for the teaching of a poem/song, "The Hands," and a mariachi piece, "Son." A list of print music resources and a discography are provided.

422. *Olson, Dale A., and Selwyn Ahyoung. "Latin America and the Caribbean," in *Multicultural Perspectives in Music Education*, edited by William M. Anderson and Patricia Shehan Campbell, 79–118. Reston, VA: Music Educators National Conference, 1989. Grades 6+.

    This resource provides good coverage of the people and music of Latin America and the Caribbean and has seven lesson plans on teaching music and instruments, including Spanish-, African-, and Indian-derived traditions. Topics include making and playing an Andean panpipe; rhythmic drum patterns; Afro-Latin American instruments and songs; calypso and steel band music from Trinidad and Tobago; the Spanish guitar; and *salsa* music. A bibliography, discography, filmography, and map are provided.

 Book

423. *Horton, Judith Page, ed. *Latin American Art and Music: A Handbook for Teaching*. Institute of Latin American Studies, 1989. (The University of Texas at Austin, Sid. W. Richardson Hall, Austin, TX 78712) 174pp. Grades 4+. [ED 342705]

    This collection of essays, curriculum units, and study guides includes a good section on the musical heritage of Latin America. See especially the following sections: "The Study of Latin American Folk Music and the Classroom" and "La Bamba: Reflections of Many People." Bibliographies and discographies are included.

♪ Recordings

424. *Discovering the Music of Latin America.* AMS Media. (9710 DeSoto Ave., Chatsworth, CA 91311-4409) videocassette, 20 min., color. Grades 3–6.

This video presents music, ranging from pre-Columbian to modern, with ancient, folk, and modern instruments. Dance music is also represented with several folk dances from different countries and a discussion of several dance rhythms, including the tango, rumba, and bossa nova.

425. *Music of Latin America: Mexico, Ecuador, Brazil.* Sounds of the World series. Music Educators National Conference, Reston, VA, 1987. 3 audiocassettes.

This set of cassettes contains interviews and music recorded in the United States by Mexican, Ecuadorian, and Brazilian immigrants. Suggestions on how to teach music selections in the classroom and study guides are included.

426. *Teaching the Music of Hispanic Americans.* Music Educators National Conference, Reston, VA, 1991. videocassette, 26 min., color.

Ethnomusicologists Dale A. Olson and David E. Sheely discuss the development of Hispanic American music, including a demonstration of Andean raft pipes and Mexican mariachi. A teacher's guide is provided.

427. *JVC/Smithsonian Folkways Video Anthology of Music and Dance of the Americas, vol. 4: The Caribbean.* Multicultural Media, Montpelier, VT, 1995. videocassette, 58 min., color.

A large number of short segments of dance and music that reflect the variety of music cultures of the region are presented in this video. A 59-page booklet is included containing an overview essay, selection descriptions, a list of resource material, and suggested activities.

428. *JVC/Smithsonian Folkways Video Anthology of Music and Dance of the Americas, vol. 5: Central and South America.* Multicultural Media, Montpelier, VT, 1995. videocassette, 53 min., color.

General features of Latin American music are explored here with selected performances of music and dance from Belize, Brazil, Chile, Colombia, Guatemala, and Guyana. A 42-page booklet is included, with overview essay, selection descriptions, a list of resource materials, and suggested activities.

Further Sources of Songs

429. Orozca, Jose-Luis. *De Colores and Other Latin American Folk Songs for Children.* New York: Dutton Children's Books, 1994. 56pp. Arr. for guitar and piano.
    This colorfully illustrated songbook contains 27 songs in Spanish with English translations, each with a brief introduction. A subject index is included.

430. Silverman, Jerry. *Mel Bay Presents Songs of Latin America.* Pacific, MO: Mel Bay, 1994. 87pp. Arr. for guitar and piano. [P]
    This is a collection of folksongs from 19 countries, presented in Spanish with English translations.

431. ———. *Mel Bay Presents Songs of Mexico.* Pacific, MO: Mel Bay, 1994. 79pp. Arr. for guitar and piano. [P]
    This collection contains 31 Mexican folksongs in Spanish and English. The songs cover such subjects as social and economic conditions, migrant workers, and occupations.

Further Reading

432. "Teaching the Music of Hispanic Americans," in *Teaching Music with a Multicultural Approach*, edited by William M. Anderson, 65–86. Reston, VA: Music Educators National Conference, 1991. [P] Grades 7+.
    This brief article covers Mexican *mestizo* music, Afro-Cuban music, and music from Latin America. A lesson plan for making Peruvian and Bolivian raft pipes and a list of selected resources are provided.

Puerto Rico

433. Perez-Selles, Marla E., ed. *Building Bridges of Learning and Understanding: A Collection of Classroom Activities on Puerto Rican Culture.* Andover, MA: Network Regional Laboratory for Educational Improvement of the Northeast & Islands. n.d. [ED 328636]
    This publication is a compilation of 35 activities that integrate elements of Puerto Rican history and culture into selected areas of K-8 curriculum. Included are lesson plans for identifying Tiano Indian musical instruments, making classroom versions of such instruments, and information on traditional Christmas season music. Worksheets are also provided.

Middle East

(See also World Cultures: General)

♪ Articles

434. Campbell, Patricia Shehan. "Bruno Nettl on Music of Islam," *Music Educators Journal* 81, no. 3 (November 1994): 19–25.
    In this interview, a noted ethnomusicologist comments on the cultural and historical context of songs and music-making in Iran and the Middle East. A lesson plan for the teaching of a song and a short list of music resources on the subject are also given. A bibliography and discography are provided.

435. Sawa, George D. "The Middle East," in *Multicultural Perspectives in Music Education*, edited by William M. Anderson and Patricia S. Campbell, 281–94. Reston, VA: Music Educators National Conference, 1989. Grades 7+.
    This is a good introduction to the cultures and music of the Middle East. Seven lesson plans are given that cover rhythms, use of tambourines, and instruments. A bibliography, discography, filmography, and map are included.

Recordings

436. For films and recordings of music from the Middle East, see Ellen Fairbanks Rodman, ed. *World of Islam, Images and Echoes: A Critical Guide to Films and Recordings*. Islamic Teaching Materials Project, Unit #7. New York: American Council of Learned Societies, 1980. (228 East 45th Street, 16th Floor, New York, NY 10017)

437. *Discovering the Music of the Middle East*. AMS Media. (9710 DeSoto Ave., Chatsworth, CA 91311-4409) videocassette, 20 min., color. Grades 3–6.
    This video presents performances of Middle Eastern music on such instruments as the *oud, sanur, qanun, cimbalon*, and *dumbeck* as well as several Middle Eastern dances. A brief but useful lesson guide is also included.

438. *Music of the Middle East: Arabian, Persian/Iranian and Turkish*. Music Educators National Conference, Reston, VA, 1990. 3 videocassettes.
    These three tapes include interviews and performances by refugees from the Middle East now living in the United States and come with a teacher's guide with transcriptions for some of the music.

AUTHOR/TITLE INDEX

Numbers refer to entry number.

African Americans, 60
Ahyoung, Selwyn, 422
Allen, William Francis, 142
Alloy, Evelyn, 233
Almanac of New England Farm Songs, An, 225, 268
America in song, 78
American Folksongs of Protest, 74, 146, 217, 228, 237, 242
American History in Ballad and Song, 84
American Indian Music for the Classroom, 201
American Industrial Ballads, 209
American Labor Songs of the 19th Century, 216
American Music, 243
American Origins of 'Yankee Doodle,' 110
American Patchwork: Appalachian Journey, 275
American Patchwork: The Land Where the Blues Began, 63, 275
American Revolution Through Its Songs and Ballads, 103
American Songbag, 90
Anastasio, Joseph L., 149
Ancient Ballads Traditionally Sung in New England, 271
Anderson, William M., 377, 394, 395, 396
Animal Folk Songs for Children, 25, 31
Anthony Seeger on Music of Amazonian Indians, 420
Arithmetic Teacher, 15
Arlen, Karen W., 290
Arnett, Hazel, 88
Arnold, Byron, 287
Arts As Education, 7

Ballad of America: The History of the United States in Song and Story, 81
Ballad Makin' in the Mountains of Kentucky, 300
Ballads and Broadsides of the Revolution, 112
Ballads and Folk Songs of the Southwest, 280
Ballads and Songs Collected by the Missouri Folklore Society, 312
Ballads and Songs from Ohio, 327
Ballads and Songs from Utah, 335
Ballads and Songs of the Civil War, 152
Ballads and Songs of Indiana, 295
Ballads and Songs of Southern Michigan, 309
Ballads and Songs of the Shantyboy, 310
Ballads Migrant in New England, 272
Ballads of the Kentucky Highlands, 298
Ballads of the War of 1812, 118
Ballard, Louis W., 197, 201
Barry, Phillips, 231, 303, 304, 338
Barton, Cathy, 157
Bay State Ballads, 308
Beat of the Band, 45, 50
Beggs-Cass, Barbara, 191
Belden, H. M., 312
Bell Yung on the Music of China, 393
Benson, John, 248
Beyer, Jack, 14
Birds, Beasts, Bugs and Little Fishes, 26
Birds, Waves, and Squeaky Grass, 32
Black Experience As Expressed Through Music, 64
Blues and the Grays: Songs of the Civil War, 162
Body, Boots, & Britches, 320
Boette, Marie, 345

111

Bonyun, Bill, 103, 156, 210, 246, 256, 270, 369
Bonyun, Gene, 270
Bowman, Kent H., 108, 121, 160
Brand, Oscar, 190
Brewster, Paul, 295
British Ballads from Maine, 304
Britsch, Barbara M., 53
Broadsides and Their Music in Colonial America, 97
Brother, Can You Spare a Dime?, 164
Brown, Frank C., 322
Brown, George, 337, 338
Brown, Sheldon, 172
Bruno Nettle on Music of Islam, 434
Building Bridges of Learning and Understanding: A Collection of Classroom Activities on Puerto Rican Culture, 433
Burl Ives Song Book, 80
Burton, Thomas G., 333
Bush, Michael E., 346

Canada's Story in Song, 403
Canaller's Songbook, 352
Cansler, Loman D., 314
Callinan, Tom, 38
Campbell, Patricia Shehan, 58, 60, 198, 199, 274, 378, 379, 393, 394, 408, 420, 421, 434
Carawan, Candie, 177
Carawan, Guy, 177
Carey, George, 307
Carpenter, Ann Miller, 360
Carry It On: The Story of America's Working People in Song and Picture, 215
Cash, Johnny, 358
Cazden, Norman, 318
Century of Liberty and War Songs, 108, 121, 160
Chanterelle, 138
Chanterelle: French in America, 138
Chantying Aboard American Ships, 251
Chapin, Tom, 39
Cheyney, Thomas, 334
Chickering, Graldine J., 309
Chilcoat, George W., 140, 185
Children's Jukebox: A Subject Guide to Musical Recordings and Programming Ideas for Songsters,
 Ages 1–12, 6, 30, 44, 50, 214, 222, 226, 350
Circling the Glode: Multicultural Resources, 376
Civil War, 154
Civil War History, 163
Civil War Songs, 155
Civil War Through Its Songs and Ballads, 156
Clarinet, the Washtub, and the Musical Nails: How Musical Instruments Work, 47
Clark, Elizabeth, 49
Clayton, Paul, 230, 245, 308, 344, 368
Cline, Dallas, 52, 54
Cockburn, Victor, 7, 386
Coe, Donna L., 2
Coffin, Tristram Potter, 109
Cohen, David, 129, 284
Cohen, Norm, 313, 361
Colcord, Joanna, 249, 370
Colonial and Revolutionary Songs, 94, 104, 119
Come All You Coal Miners, 240
Connecticut's Music in the Revolutionary Era, 113
Contentment, or, The Compleat Nutmeg-State Songster, 291
Conversations with David P. McAllester on Navajo Music, 198
Cooper, B. Lee, 174, 175, 176
Cotton Mill Girls, 236
Courlander, Harold, 72, 144, 288
Cowboy and Western Songs: A Comprehensive Anthology, 221
Cowboy Ballads, 219
Cowboy Songs, 220
Cox, John Harrington, 347
Cultural Consciousness in Teaching General Music, 377

Daly, Cindy L., 79
Daniels, Elva S., 78, 207
Davis, Arthur Kyle, Jr., 341, 342
Days of '49: Songs of the Gold Rush, 135
Demas, Alex, 236
Dennison-Tansey, Amy, 53
Depression and New Deal Through Songs and Ballads, 165
Depression and World War II As Seen Through Country Music, 172

De Colores and Other Latin American Folk Songs, 429
DesRosiers, Mary, 266
Devil's Ditties, 301
Dhand, Harry, 402
Diamond Bessie and the Shepards, 360
DiSavino, Liza, 43
Discovering American Indian Music, 204
Discovering Jazz, 65
Discovering the Music of India, 418
Discovering the Music of Japan, 397
Discovering the Music of Latin America, 424
Discovering the Music of the Middle East, 437
Doerflinger, William Main, 323, 250
Dolph, Edward Arthur, 254
Douglas, Jim, 234, 235, 267, 269, 291
Down in a Coal Mine, 241
Dust Bowl Ballads, 166
Dwyer, Richard A., 129, 133, 284
Dyer, Bob, 157

Early American Songbook, 96, 107
Earthy Songs, 37
East Tennessee State University Collection of Folklore: Folksongs, 333
Echoes of America, 66, 276
Eckstorm, Fannie Hardy, 304, 305
Eddy, Mary, 327
Election Songs of the United States, 190
Ella Jenkins' Multicultural Children's Songs, 383
English, Logan, 135
English Folk Songs from the Southern Appalachians, 279
Europe, 408
Everybody Says Freedom, 178

Farewell to Eirinn, 137
Farmers of the Plains and Prairies: Their Story in Song, 1850's–1880's, 224, 264
Farucci, Samuel L., 91
Federal Period, 1786–1801, 114, 187
Fife, Alta S., 221
Fife, Austin E., 221
Fifty Sail on Newburgh Bay, 321
Fink, Cathy, 56

Fit Music into the Study of Fractions, 21
Flanders, Helen Harkness, 271, 272, 337, 338
Fo'c'sle Songs and Shanties, 245, 368
Folk Ballads from North Carolina, 322
Folk Song History of America, 91
Folk Song in South Carolina, 332
Folk Song, U.S.A., 89
Folk Songs and Singing Games of the Illinois Ozarks, 294
Folk Songs from the West Virginia Hills, 348
Folk Songs of Canada, 407
Folk Songs of Central West Virginia, 346
Folk Songs of Colonial Times, 93
Folk Songs of Idaho and Utah, 293, 336
Folk Songs of Maine, 306
Folk Songs of North America, 70, 130, 213, 259
Folk Songs of Old New England, 273
Folk Songs of the Catskills, 318
Folk Songs of the Great Lakes Region, 260
Folk Songs of the Kentucky Mountains, 299
Folk Songs of the World, 387
Folk Songs of Virginia, 341
Folk Songs Out of Wisconsin, 349
Folksong in the Classroom, 23, 24, 35, 93, 101, 102, 114, 115, 123, 134, 136, 140, 153, 165, 187, 188, 218, 224, 229, 239, 244, 253, 255, 264, 373, 404, 409
Folksongs and Ballads of Virginia, 344
Folksongs Mainly from West Virginia, 347
Folksongs of Alabama, 287
Folksongs of Florida, 292
Folksongs of Mississippi, 311
Folksongs of Vermont, 340
Foner, Philip S., 216
For the Beauty of the Earth, 43
Fowke, Edith, 170, 212, 403, 407
Fowls of the Air: Wild and Domesticated, 24
Freilicher, Elizabeth, 372
From Farm to Factory: The Story of the New England Textile Industry in Song, 234
Frontier Ballads, 124
Fuson, Henry H., 298

Gainer, Patrick, 348
Gardner, Emelyn E., 309
Garland, Trudi Hammel, 17
Garrison, Lucy McKim, 142
Garson, Eugenia, 262
George, Luvenia A., 59, 73
Glass, Paul, 61, 150, 202
Glazer, Joe, 170, 212, 241
Glazer, Tom, 86, 128, 154, 159, 173
Godfrey, Margaret, 21
Goines, Dr. Leonard, 145
Golden Age of Whaling in New England, 258
Golden Eagle String Band, 320, 352, 354
Goy, Barbara, 14
Grand Canal Ballads, 354
Great American Work Songs, 207
Green, Archie, 241
Greenway, John, 74, 146, 217, 228, 237, 242
Grimes, Anne, 328
Guthrie, Woody, 166, 171

Hard Hitting Songs for Hard-Hit People, 171
Harlow, Frederick Pease, 251
Harris, Kim, 141
Harris, Reggie, 141
Hawes, Bessie Lomax, 69
Heaps, Porter W., 161
Heaps, Willard A., 161
Henry, Mellinger, 323
Here's to the Women: 100 Songs for and About American Women, 372
Hewitt, Nat, 266
Heywood, Charles, 387
Hispanic Folk Songs of New Mexico, 316
History Alive Through Music: Musical Memories of Laura Ingalls Wilder, 265
Holiday Songbook, 193
Holiday Songs Around the World, 194
Holidays and Special Days: A Sourcebook of Songs, Rhymes and Movement for Each Month of the Elementary School Year, 194
Homemade Instruments, 55
Hopton-Jones, Pamela, 389
Horton, Judith Page, 423
House, Wallace, 118
Houston, Cisco, 219
Hubbard, Lester A., 335
Hudson, Arthur Palmer, 311
Hughes, Robert, 339
Hugill, Stan, 252, 371
Hullfish, William, 352
Hunter, Ilene, 55
Huntington, Gale, 258

I Hear America Singing!, 88
Images of Vietnam: A Popular Music Approach, 185
India/South India, 419
Insights into American History Through Folk Songs, 85
Instructor, 32, 49, 78, 207
Integrating Music with Other Studies, 20, 22, 186
Integrating Music, Reading, and Writing at the Primary Level, 9
Integrating Social Studies and Folk Music, 79
Introducing the Music of East Africa, 389
Irish Immigration Through Its Songs and Ballads, 136
Ives, Burl, 80
Ives, Sandy, 306

Jefferson, Madison and the War of 1812, (1801–1814), 117
Jessup, Lynne, 380
Jewish People of Eastern Europe Through Their Songs and Ballads, 409
John Brown's Body, 163
Johnny Whistlerigger/Rebel in the Woods: Civil War Songs from the Western Border, 157
Johnston, Richard, 407
Joiner, Charles, 332
Jones, Arthur C., 75, 147
Jones, Bessie, 69
Journal of Geography, 122, 223, 263
Judson, Marilyn, 55
JVC Video Anthology of World Music and Dance, 384
JVC/Smithsonian Folkways Video Anthology of Music and Dance: Africa, 392

JVC/Smithsonian Folkways Video Anthology of Music and Dance: Central and South America, 428
JVC Video Anthology of World Music and Dance: East Asia III, China 1, 384
JVC Video Anthology of World Music and Dance: East Asia IV, China 2, 384
JVC Video Anthology of World Music and Dance: East Asia V, China 3, Mongolia, 384
JVC Video Anthology of World Music and Dance: East Asia I, Korea 1, 384
JVC Video Anthology of World Music and Dance: East Asia II, Korea 2, 384
JVC Video Anthology of World Music and Dance: Europe I, Ireland, England, France, Switzerland, West Germany, Spain, Italy, Greece, 385
JVC Video Anthology of World Music and Dance: Europe II, Poland, Czechoslovakia, Hungary, 385
JVC Video Anthology of World Music and Dance: Europe II, Romania, Yugoslavia, Bulgaria, Albania, 385
JVC Video Anthology of World Music and Dance: Middle East III, Chad, Cameroon, 385
JVC Video Anthology of World Music and Dance: Middle East and Africa II, Egypt, Tunisia, Morocco, Mali, Cameroon, Zaire, Tunisia, 385
JVC Video Anthology of World Music and Dance: Middle East IV, Ivory Coast, Botswana, Republic of South Africa, 385
JVC Video Anthology of World Music and Dance: Middle East and Africa I, Turkey, Iran, Iraq, Lebanon, Qatar, 385
JVC Video Anthology of World Music and Dance: Oceania I, Micronesia, Melanesia, 386
JVC Video Anthology of World Music and Dance: Oceania II Polynesia, New Zealand, 386
JVC Video Anthology of World Music and Dance: Southeast Asia IV, Indonesia 1, 385
JVC Video Anthology of World Music and Dance: Southeast Asia V, Indonesia 2, 385
JVC Video Anthology of World Music and Dance: Southeast Asia III, Malaysia, Philippines, 384
JVC Video Anthology of World Music and Dance: Southeast Asia II, Thailand, Burma, 384
JVC Video Anthology of World Music and Dance: Southeast Asia I, Vietnam, Cambodia, 384
JVC Video Anthology of World Music and Dance: South Asia I, India 1, 385
JVC Video Anthology of World Music and Dance: South Asia II, India 2, 385
JVC Video Anthology of World Music and Dance: South Asia III, India 3, 385
JVC Video Anthology of World Music and Dance: South Asia IV, Pakistan, Bangladesh, 385
JVC Video Anthology of World Music and Dance: South Asia V, Sri Lanka, Nepal, Bhutan, 385
JVC Video Anthology of World Music and Dance: Soviet Union III, Azerbaijan, Armenia, Georgia, Dagestan, 385
JVC Video Anthology of World Music and Dance: Soviet Union IV, Kazakh, Uzbek, Turkmen, Tajik, Kirgiz, Kalmyk, Mari, Bashkir, Siberia, 385
JVC Video Anthology of World Music and Dance: Soviet Union II, Latvia, Estonia, Lithuania, Belorussia, Ukraine, Moldavia, 385
JVC Video Anthology of World Music and Dance: Soviet Union I, Russia, 385

JVC Video Anthology of World Music and Dance: The Americas II, Mexico, Cuba, Bolivia, Argentina, 386
JVC Video Anthology of World Music and Dance: The Americas I, North American Indians, 385
JVC/Smithsonian Folkways Video Anthology of Music and Dance: The Americas, 405
JVC/Smithsonian Folkways Video Anthology of Music and Dance: The Caribbean, 427
JVC/Smithsonian Folkways Video Anthology of Music and Dance: Europe, 416
Just Listen to This Song I'm Singing: African American History Through Song, 62

Kahn, Charity Vaughn, 17
Kandall, Leslie, 8
Karpeles, Maud, 279
Keane, Delores, 137
Killen, Louis, 248
Knight, Elizabeth, 374
Koetting, James T., 77
Korson, George, 329, 330
Kracht, James B., 122, 223, 263, 366
Kreek, Esther, 126
Krone, Beatrice Perham, 483, 203, 381
Kuo-Huang, Han, 395

Langfit, Diane, 9
Latin American and the Caribbean, 422
Latin American Art and Music: A Handbook for Teaching, 423
Laura Ingalls Wilder Songbook: Favorite Songs from the "Little House" Books, 262
Lawrence, Vera Brodsky, 92
Lemay, J. A. Leo, 110
Let's Clean Up Our Act: Songs for the Earth, 38
Levene, Donna B., 3
Levine, Laurence W., 148
Liang, Minguye, 401
Lindquist, Barbara Reeder, 390, 391
Lingenfelter, Richard E., 129, 133, 284
Linscott, Eloise Hubbard, 273
List, Lynne K., 5, 11, 18, 46

Literature and Music As Resources for Social Studies, 4, 83, 203, 381
Little Music on the Prairie: Music From the Books of Laura Ingalls Wilder, 266
Lomax, Alan, 70, 89, 130, 171, 212
Lomax, John A., 89, 259
Long Steel Rail: The Railroad in American Folksong, 361
Lonnquist, Ken, 37
Louisiana French Folk Songs, 302
Lord, Donald C., 139
Lumbering—Cutting Down the White Pine: The Shantyboys and the White River Men, 229
Lyrical Life Science, 27, 28

MacArthur, Margaret, 12, 195, 225, 268, 340
MacColl, Ewan, 257
Maine Woods Songster, 231, 303
Making and Playing Homemade Musical Instruments, 56
Making Simple Folk Instruments for Children, 52
Manning, Ambrose N., 333
Maryland Folk Legends and Songs, 307
Marxer, Marcie, 56
Masyga, Jean, 32
Math and Music: Harmonious Connections, 17
Matteson, Maurice, 323
May, Elizabeth, 388
McAllester, David P., 200, 206
McCullough-Brabson, Ellen, 274, 379
McGill, Josephine, 299
McIntosh, David, 294
McNeil, Keith, 85, 94, 104, 119, 125, 155, 211, 220, 359
McNeil, Rusty, 85, 94, 104, 119, 125, 155, 211, 220, 359
Measure of Music, 16
Mel Bay Presents Songs of England, 411
Mel Bay Presents Songs of France, 412
Mel Bay Presents Songs of Germany, 413
Mel Bay Presents Songs of Ireland, 414
Mel Bay Presents Songs of Latin America, 430
Mel Bay Presents Songs of Mexico, 431
Mel Bay Presents Songs of Scotland, 415

Mel Bay Presents Songs of the British Isles, 410
Mel Pay Presents the American History Songbook, 82
Mellonee Burnim on African American Music, 58
Mendelsohn, Esther L., 19
Middle East, 435
Mills, Alan, 247, 403, 406
Mine, Mill and Tunnel Workers, 1877–1932, 239
Minstrels of the Mine Patch, 329
Minstrelsy of Maine, 305
Minton, John, 238
Missouri Folk Songs, 314
Moore, Chauncy O., 280
Moore, Ethel, 280
More Traditional Ballads of Virginia, 342
Mormon Songs from the Rocky Mountains, 334
Morris, Alton, 292
Moser, Artus, 326
Moses, Barbara, 15
Mother Earth, 39
Mountain Minstrelsy of Pennsylvania, 331
Moving West, 125
Mulligan, Mary Ann, 1, 20, 22, 186
Multicultural Perspectives in Music Education, 60, 199, 274, 390, 394, 395, 408, 422, 435
Murdock, Lee, 260
Music and the Underground Railroad, 141
Music, Art & Drama Experiences for the Elementary Classroom, 5, 11, 18, 46
Music Educators Journal, 14, 52, 197, 198, 376, 389, 393, 420, 421, 434
Music for Patriots, Politicians, and Presidents: Harmonies and Discords of the First Hundred Years, 92
Music in Colonial Massachusetts, 1630–1820. 97, 111
Music in the Old Time Way: Traditional Music and Musicians from the Southern Appalachians, 277
Music in the Southwest, 281
Music of Black Americans: A History, 76
Music of East Asia: Chinese, Korean and Japanese, 398
Music of Latin America: Mexico, Ecuador, and Brazil, 425
Music of the Billions, 401
Music of the Middle East, 438
Music of Southeast Asia: Lao, Hmong, and Vietnamese, 399
Music of Worship, Music of Work, Music of Play: The Blues, 77
Music: Program Notes, 10
Music Through Children's Literature: Theme and Variations, 3
Musical Calendar of Festivals: Folk Songs of Feast-Days and Holidays from Around the World, 191
Musical Heritage of America, 86
Musical Reflections of Canada's History, 402
Musics of Many Cultures: An Introduction, 388
My First Music Video: A Kids' Guide for Fun to Make Musical Instruments, 57

Nash, Grace C., 192
Native Americans of the Southwest, 199
Nature Nuts, 40
Negro Folk Music, U.S.A, 72, 144
Negro Songs from Alabama, 288
New England Textile Industry Through Its Songs, 235
New Green Mountain Songster, 338
New Lost City Ramblers, 168
North America/Native America, 206
North Carolina Ballads, 326

O Canada: A History of Canada in Song, 406
Oh Empty Set! Oh Empty Set!, 14
Oh! That Low Bridge: Songs of the Erie Canal, 355
Ohio State Ballads, 328
Olney, Marguerite, 271
Olson, Dale A., 422
One Voice: Music and Stories in the Classroom, 53
Open sets, 14

Original "Talking Union," with the Almanac Singers and Other Union Songs with Pete Seeger and Chorus, 167
Ozark Folksongs, 313
Ozorca, Jose-Luis, 429

Para, Dave, 157
Peddler's Pack, 269
Pennsylvania Songs and Legends, 330
Perceptions of the Great Plains in Nineteenth Century Folk Song: Teaching About Place, 122, 223, 263
Perez-Selles, Marla E., 433
Peters, Harry B., 349
Piggyback Planet: Songs for a Whole Earth, 41
Pirtle, Sarah, 42
Play-Party in Indiana, 295
Popular Music Handbook, The: A Resource Guide for Teachers, Librarians and Media Specialists, 174
Popular Songs, Military Conflicts, and Public Perceptions of the United States at War, 175
Project I-C-E, Music K-3, Environmental Education Guide, 33
Project I-C-E, Music 4-6, Environmental Education Guide, 34
Proudfit, Linda, 15
Put American Indian Music in the Classroom, 197

Rabson, Carolyn, 106
Railroads in American Folksong, 1865–1920, 360
Railroads: Their History, People & Songs, 356
Randolph, Vance, 313
Rapley, Janice, 192
Reading Teacher, 9
Reagon, Bernice Johnson, 59
Reck, David B., 419
Reconstruction Era: The Night They Drove Old Dixie Down, 149
Reid, Bob, 6, 30, 44, 50, 214, 222, 226, 350
Reiser, Robert S., 215
Reneham, Ed, 321

Resource Guide to Themes in Contemporary American Song Lyrics, 1950–1985, 176
Rickaby, Franz, 310
Ridin' the Rail: The Great American Train Story, 358
Riley, Margaret C., 2
Riley, Martha Chrisman, 297
Ring Games of Alabama, 289
Ritz-Salmein, Dianne, 10
Rivers of America, Part I & II, 35
Robb, John, 316
Robinson, Earl, 131, 283
Rogers, Sally, 41
Roll and Go: The Shantyman's Day Aboard a Yankee Clipper, 246, 369
Roots and Branches: A Legacy of Multicultural Music for Children, 379
Rothenberg, Barbara Skolnick, 16
Rubin, Ruth, 409

Sandburg, Carl, 90
Sanger, Kerran L., 184
Sawa, George D., 435
Sawyers, June Skinner, 162
Scarborough, Dorothy, 324, 343
Schrader, Arthur, 111
Schupman, Edwin, 200
School Library Media Activities Monthly, 164
Science and Children, 45, 50
Science and Music, 48
Scott, John A., 3, 24, 25, 36, 81, 93, 101, 102, 103, 112, 114, 115, 117, 123, 134, 136, 153, 165, 187, 188, 218, 224, 229, 235, 239, 244, 255, 264, 356, 362, 367, 373, 404, 409
Scott, John W., 24, 404
Seed That Grew, 49
Seeger, Mike, 25
Seeger, Peggy, 25, 257
Seeger, Pete, 26, 124, 171, 178, 209, 215, 321
Seeger, Ruth C., 31
Seidman, Laurence, 23, 24, 35, 36, 93, 98, 101, 102, 111, 115, 117, 123, 134, 165, 187, 188, 218, 224, 229, 239, 244, 255, 264, 356, 362, 367, 373, 404, 409

Shanties from the Seven Seas, 252, 371
Shapiro, Ann, 38
Sharp, Cecil J., 279
Sharrow, Gregory, 112, 195
Shoemaker, Henry, 331
Silber, Irwin, 99, 116, 120, 131, 151, 153, 189, 283
Silverman, Jerry, 62, 71, 82, 100, 132, 143, 152, 179, 193, 208, 286, 353, 357, 363, 365, 410, 411, 412, 413, 414, 415, 430, 431
Simple Folk Instruments to Make and Play, 56
Sing for Freedom: The Story of the Civil Rights Movement Through Its Songs, 177, 180
Sing Out!, 112, 145, 162
Sing the Earth: A Farming and Gardening Songbook, 227
Singa Hipsy Doodle and Other Folk Songs of West Virginia, 345
Singing Indiana History: A Musical Resource Guide for Teachers, 296
Singing Sixties: The Spirit of the Civil War Days Drawn from the Music of the Times, 161
Singing Soldiers: A History of the Civil War in Song, 150
Slave Song As Historical Source, The, 139
Slave Songs, 143
Slave Songs and Slave Consciousness: An Exploration of Neglected Sources, 148
Slave Songs of the United States, 142
Slobin, Mark, 77
Smith, Carleton Sprague, 97
Smyth, Mary Winslow, 304, 305
Social Education, 98, 139, 172, 175, 185, 402
Songbook of the American Revolution, 106
Song Catcher in Southern Mountains: American Folk Songs of British Ancestry, 324, 343
Songs About Animals and Other Living Creatures, 23
Songs About Our Earth and Ecology: A Celebration of Nature and Its Defense, 36
Songs About Work, Eassays in Occupational Cultures for Richard A. Reuss, 238

Songs America Voted By, 189
Songs and Stories from the American Revolution, 100
Songs and Stories of Afro-Americans, 61
Songs and Stories of the North American Indians, 202
Songs from the Depression, 168
Songs from the Hills of Vermont, 339
Songs of American Sailormen, 249, 370
Songs of Independence, 99, 116, 120
Songs of New England: A Resource Book for Teachers, 267
Songs of Newfoundland, 404
Songs of Peace, Freedom and Protest, 173
Songs of Protest and Civil Rights, 179
Songs of Soldiers, 253
Songs of the American Cowboy, 218
Songs of the American People, 286
Songs of the American Revolution, 101, 102
Songs of the American West, 129, 284
Songs of the California Gold Rush, 134
Songs of the Civil War, 151, 153, 158
Songs of the Gold Rush, 133
Songs of the Great American West, 131, 283
Songs of the Great Lakes, 261
Songs of the Sailor and Lumberman, 232, 250
Songs of the Sea, 247
Songs of the Sea: Chanties, Fo'c'sle and Fishing Songs, 244, 367
Songs of the Sea, Rivers, Lakes and Canals, 353, 363
Songs of the Suffragettes, 374
Songs of the Western Frontier, 132
Songs of Work and Protest, 170, 212
Songs of Yankee Whaling, 256
Songs the Whalemen Sang, 258
Songs to Cultivate the Sensations of Freedom, 111
Sorrels, Rosalie, 293, 336
Sound Off! Soldier Songs, 254
Sounds of the World, 385
Sounds of the World: Music of East Asia, 398
Sounds of the World: Music of Latin America, 425
Sounds of the World: Music of Southeast Asia, 399

Source Book of African and Afro-American Materials for Music Educators, 391
Source of African-American Music, 73
Southeast Asia, 394
Southern, Eileen, 76
Southern Appalachian Mountains, 274
Southern Textile Song Tradition Reconsidered, 238
Spanish Folk Songs of New Mexico, 317
Spanish Folk Songs of the Southwest, 282
Standifer, James A., 60, 274, 390
Steady As She Goes, 248
Steamboatin' Days, 364
Step It Down: Games, Plays, Songs and Stories from the Afro-American Heritage, 69
Steinbergh, Judith, 386
Steven Loza on Latino music, 421
Sturgis, Edith B., 339
Stutler, Boyd B., 163
Sub-Sahara Africa, 390
Sunserl, Marylee, 29
Sutherland, Pete, 266
Swan, Howard, 281

Teacher, 21, 149
Teaching About Slavery Through Folk Song, 140
Teaching About the American Revolution Through Its Folk Songs, 98
Teaching Children Mathematics, 16
Teaching Music with a Multicultural Approach, 59, 73, 200, 396, 432
Teaching Primary Math with Music: Grades K-3, 19
Teaching the Music of African-Americans, 59, 67
Teaching the Music of Asian Americans, 396, 400
Teaching the Music of Hispanic Americans, 426, 432
Teaching the Music of the American Indians, 200, 205
They Came Singing: Songs from California's History, 290
Thomas, Jean, 300, 301
Tipple, Loom & Rail: Songs of the Industrialization of the South, 278

Titon, Jeff Todd, 77
Tooze, Ruth, 4, 83, 203, 381
Touch the Past: A Musical Diary of a Pioneer Family's Journey West, 126
Traditional American Folk Songs from the Anne & Frank Warner Collection, 315, 319, 325
Traditional Songs of Singing Cultures: A World Sampler, 378
Train Songs, 357
Transportation, 351
Traugh, Steven, 87, 95, 105, 127
Treasury of Civil War Songs, 159
Trimillos, Ricardo, 395
Trouble in the Mines: A History in Song and Story by Women of Appalachia, 243
Tucker, Judith Cook, 376, 379
Twenty-Nine Beech Mountain Folk Songs and Ballads, 323
Two Hands Hold the Earth, 42
Tryin' to Get Home, 68

Uncertain Glory, 109
U.S. Constitution Through Its Songs and Ballads, 115, 188
Uses of Folk Music and Songwriting in the Classroom, 7

Van Alstine, Gladys, 32
Van Stone, Mary, 282, 317
Van Winkle Keller, Kate, 113
Vermont Folksongs and Ballads, 337
Vermont Heritage Songbook, 12, 195
Vinson, Lee, 96, 107
Voices of American History, 87, 95, 105, 127
Voices of the Civil Rights Movement: Black American Freedom Songs, 1955–1965, 181

Wade in the Water, 75, 147
'Walk Over!': Music in the Slave Narratives, 145
Ward, George, 355
Ware, Charles Pickard, 142
Warner, Anne, 315, 319, 325
Warner, Frank, 156
Warner, Gerret, 248

Warner, Jeff, 248
We Write the Songs, 8
Webber, Mary, 13, 196
Wenner, Hilda E., 372
We Shall Overcome, 182
We Shall Overcome: Songs of the Freedom Riders and the Sit-Ins, 183
Western Railroad Songs, 359
Westward Movement: The Pioneers, the Indians and the Frontier, 123
Whale Watching, 29
Whaler Out of New Bedford, 257
Wheeler, Mary, 364
When the Spirit Says Sing!, 184
Where I Come From! Songs and Poems from Many Cultures, 386
Whitefield, Irene, 302
Who Built America: American History Through Its Folk Songs, 210
Whole Language: Discovery Activites for the Primary Grades, 2
William and Mary Quarterly, 110
Wilson, Ruth Mack, 113
Winning of the West, 128
Wolford, Leah Jackson, 297

Women's Songs, 373
Woody Guthrie, 169
Work Songs, 71, 208
Working and Union, 211
Working Women's Music: The Songs and Struggles of Women in the Cotton Mills, Textile Plants and Needle Trades, 233
World of Islam, Images and Echoes: A Critical Guide to Films and Recordings, 436
World Music: A Source Book for Teaching, 380
Worlds of Music: An Introduction to the Music of the World's Peoples, 77, 149
Worlds of Music: East Europe, Albanian, Greek and South Slavic, 417
Worth Ten Men on a Rope, 366
Writing Ballads From Local Historical Legends, 13, 196

Yankee Legend, 270
Yurchenco, Henrietta, 243

SUBJECT INDEX

Reference is to entry number. Number after / refers to a subentry.

Abolitionist, 125, 212. *See also* Civil War
Addition, 18, 19
Africa, 4, 384/16–17, 389–392
African Americans, 58–77, 377
Alabama, 287–289
Albania, 384/22, 417
Algae, 27
Amazon. *See* Suya Indians
American History. *See* Colonial Period, American Revolution, Federal Period, War of 1812, Industrial Revolution, Westward Expansion, Gold Rush, Immigration, Slavery, Civil War, Reconstruction, Great Depression, World War II, Post World War II, Civil Rights Movement, Vietnam
American Revolution, 98–113
Animals, 23–31. *See also* Environment
Appalachia. *See* South
Area (Mathematics), 16
Argentina, 384/28
Armenia, 384/25
Asia, 4, 393–401
Australia, 4
Azerbaijan, 384/25

Bacteria, 27
Bangladesh, 384/14
Banjo, 66, 276
Bashkir, 384/26
Belize, 428
Belorussia, 384/24
Bhutan, 384/15
Bill of Rights, 115, 118
Birds, 24, 26, 27, 30. *See also* Environment
Blake, Eubie, 64
Blues, 60, 63, 70, 72, 77, 296. *See also* African Americans

Bolivia, 384/28
Books. *See* Literature
Brazil, 425, 428. *See also* America
British Isles, 410
Broadsides, 92, 97, 111, 112
Bulgaria, 384/22, 408
Burma, 384/7
Burns, Robert, 415

Cajun music. *See* Louisiana
California, 290. *See also* Gold Rush
Calypso, 422
Camaroon, 384/17–18
Cambodia, 384/6, 394. *See also* Asia
Canada, 4, 402–407
Canal, 352–355
Caribbean, 421–427
Carmichael, Hoagy, 296
Central America, 428. *See also* Latin America
Chad, 384/18
Chile, 428. *See also* Latin America
China, 384/3–5, 393, 395, 396, 398, 400, 401
Cimbalon, 437
City life, 174
Civil Rights Movement, 174, 177–184
Civil War, 149–163
Colonial America, 93–97
Columbia, 428. *See also* Latin America
Communication, 174–176
Composition. *See* Songwritng
Counting, 15, 19, 20
Connecticut, 113, 291
Conservation. *See* Environment
Constitution, United States, 115
Cowboys, 31, 218–222
Cuba, 67, 384/28
Czechoslovakia, 384/21

Dagestan, 384/25
Death, 174, 176
Dickens, Hazel, 243
Division (Mathematics), 19
Divorce, 176
Dogs, 30, 31
Duke Ellington, 61
Dumbeck, 437

East Asia, 384/1–5
Eastern Europe, 417. *See also* Europe
Ecology. *See* Environment
Economics, 174
Ecuador, 425
Education, 174, 176
Egypt, 384/17
Elections, 189, 190
England, 384/20, 410. *See also* British Isles
Environment, 28, 32–44, 174, 386
Erie Canal, 352, 353–355
Estonia, 384/24
Europe, 4, 384/20–22, 408–417

Family life, 176, 386
Farmer, 31, 50, 129, 223–228
Federal Period, 114–116
Fibonacci numbers, 17
Fish, 26, 30
Florida, 292
Fo'c'sle (Forecastle) songs. *See* Sailors, Ships
Fowl. *See* Birds
Fractals, 17
Fractions, 15, 16, 18, 21
France, 384/20, 412
French Canadian, 138
Frogs, 30
Frontier. *See* Westward Expansion

Game songs, 68, 69, 72
Gardening, 50, 226
Geography, 122, 186
Geometry, 19
Germany, 384/20, 413
Ghana, 390
Glazer, Joe, 217
Golden Ratio, 17
Gold Rush, 133–135

Gospel music, 58, 59, 64, 68, 72, 73.
    See also African Americans
Government, 187–190
Grammar, 11
Great Depression, 164–172
Great Lakes, 260–261
Great Plains, 223, 224, 262–266
Greece, 384/20, 417
Guatemala, 428
Gunning, Sarah Ogan, 243
Guthrie, Woody, 169, 217
Guyana, 428

Handy, W. C., 61
Hispanic Americans, 432. *See also* Latin America
History. *See* African Americans, American History, Local History, Native American, Oral History, Women's History
Holidays, 191–194
Hudson River Valley, 321
Hungary, 384/21, 408. *See also* Europe
Hunting, 31

Idaho, 293
Illinois, 294
Immigration, 125, 136–138
India, 384/11–13, 418–419
Indiana, 295–297
Indians. *See* Native American
Indonesia, 384/9–10, 394. *See also* Asia
Industrial Revolution. *See* Occupations: Mill Workers, Miners; Transportation: Canal, Railroad
Ingalls, Laura. *See* Wilder, Laura Ingalls
Insects, 30. *See also* Environment
Instruments. *See also* Sound
    Building/Making, 45, 50–57
        Andean pan pipe, 422
        Native American cow-horn, 206
        Native American water drum, 206
        one string diddley bow, 77
        slide veena, 419
        tambura, 419
    Type
        banjo, 66, 276
        cimbalon, 437
        ganun, 437
        kaen, 394

koto, 397
oud, 437
sanur, 437
shakuhachi, 395, 397
shamisen, 397
sitar, 419
xiao, 395
zheng, 395
Invertebrates, 27
Iraq, 384/16
Iran, 384/16, 434, 438. *See also* Middle East
Ireland, 384/20, 408, 414. *See also* British Isles
Irish immigration, 136, 137
Italy, 384/20
Ivory Coast, 384/19

Jackson, Aunt Molly, 217, 243
Japan, 395, 397, 398
Jazz, 60, 64, 296. *See also* African Americans

Kabuki theatre, 395
Kaen, 394
Kalmyk, 384/26
Kazakh, 384/26
Keith, Bill, 66
Kentucky, 298–301
Kiowa Indians, 298–301
Korea, 384/1–2, 398
Koto, 397

Labor Unions. *See* Unions
Land forms. *See* Geography
Language, 1–4
Language Arts, 1–13
Laos, 394
Latin America, 4, 420–432
Latvia, 384/24
Law and order, 174
Leadbelly, 61
Lebanon, 384/16
Literature, 3–6, 9
Lithuania, 384/24
Local history, 12, 13, 195, 196
Louisiana, 302
Lucas, Lazy Bill, 77
Lumbermen, 229–232

Maine, 231, 303–306
Malaysia, 384/8
Mali, 384/17
Mammals, 28. *See also* Animals
Mariachi, 426
Marriage, 176
Maryland, 307
Massachusetts, 308
Mathematics, 14–21
Measurements (Mathematical), 15, 16, 19
Mestizo music, 432
Mexican-American War, 283
Mexico, 384/28, 425, 426, 431. *See also* Latin America
Michigan, 309–310
Middle East, 384/16–19, 434–438
Mill (Textile) workers, 233–238
Miner, 129, 239–243. *See also* Gold Rush
Minstrel songs, 68
Mississippi, 311
Missouri, 312–314
Moldavia, 384/24
Money, 16
Mongolia, 384/5
Mormons, 129, 281, 285. *See also* Utah
Morocco, 384/17
Motown, 68
Munroe, Bill, 66
Music. *See* Blues, Calypso, Gospel, Jazz, Mestizo, Minstrel, Motown, Spirituals, Ragtime, Rap, Rock 'n' Roll, Song Games
Multiplication, 18, 19

Native American, 4, 197–206, 377, 384/27
Nature. *See* Environment
Navaho Indians, 198–206
Near East, 4
Nepal, 384/15
Newfoundland, 404
New England, 267–273
New Hampshire, 315
New Mexico, 316, 317
New York, 318–321
New Zealand, 384/30
Noh theatre, 395
North Carolina, 322–326

Oceania, 384/29–30
Occupations, 70, 71, 74, 89, 90, 207–258
Ohio, 327–328
Old age, 174
Open sets (Mathematics), 14, 20
Oral history, 174
Overpopulation, 174

Pakistan, 384/14
Papago Indian, 197, 202
Patriotism, 174
Pawnee Indians, 202
Patterns (Mathematical), 16
Pennsylvania, 329–331
Penmanship, 8
Perimeter, 16
Philippines, 377, 381, 384/8
Physics, 45–48
Pioneers. See Westward Expansion
Pi phat orchestra, 394
Plants, 27, 49, 50. See also Environment
Poetry. See Writing
Poland, 384/21
Pollution. See Environment
Porter, Cole, 296
Poverty, 176
Prediction (Mathematics), 20
Propaganda, 174
Proportion, 17
Protest Songs. See American History: American Revolution, Civil Rights Movement, Slavery, Civil War, Great Depression, Post World War II, Vietnam War; Occupations: General, Miner, Mill Worker; Women's History
Puerto Rico, 433

Ragtime, 60, 64, 296. See also African Americans
Railroad, 129, 356–359
Rap, 68
Reading, 5, 6, 8, 9
Reconstruction, 149–163
Reese, Florence, 243
Regions, 90, 259–285
Religion, 176
Republic of South Africa, 384/19
Riverboats, 362–364
Rivers, 35, 362–364

Rock 'n' Roll, 68
Romania, 384/22
Russia, 384/23

Sailors, 244–252. See also Ships
Sanur, 437
Science, 22–57
Scotland, 415. See also British Isles
Sea, 29. See also Ships
Seasons, 386. See also Holidays
Seeger, Pete, 66
Shamisen, 397
Shanty (work song). See Sailors, Ships
Ships, 365–371
Siberia, 384/26
Sioux Indians, 197, 202, 206
Sitar, 418
Slavery, 139–148. See also African Americans
Slave songs. See Slavery
Slide veena, 419
Social Studies, 58–438
Soldiers, 2, 53–254
Song games, 69, 289, 294
Songwriting, 7, 9, 386
Sound, 1, 17, 45, 46, 48
South (Region), 274–279
Southeast Asia, 384/6–11
Southwest (Region), 280–282
South America. See Latin America
South Asia, 384/12–15
South Carolina, 332
Soviet Union, 23–27
Spain, 384/20 408. See also Europe
Spelling, 8, 11
Spiders, 30
Spirituals, 59, 60, 64, 68, 70, 72, 73, 75. See also African Americans
Sri Lanka, 384/15
States, 286–349
Steamboats. See Riverboats
Subtraction (Mathematics), 18, 19
Suffragettes, 374
Surveys, 15
Suya Indians, 420
Sweden, 408
Switzerland, 384/20

Tajik, 384/26
Tambura, 419
Technology, 174

Subject Index / 127

Tennessee, 333
Thailand, 384/7, 394
Thompson, Odell, 66
Tiano Indians, 433
Time (Measurement), 15, 18
Tobago, 422
Trains. *See* Railroad
Transportation, 35, 176, 350–371
Trigonometric functions, 17
Trinidad, 422
Tunisia, 384/17
Turkey, 384/16, 438
Turkmen, 384/26

Underground Railroad, 141
Unemployment, 176
Ukraine, 384/24
Unions. *See* Occupations
Utah, 334–336

Vermont, 12, 195, 337–340
Vietnam, 384/6, 394–399
Vietnam War, 185
Virginia, 341–344

War. *See* American Revolution, Civil War, Mexican-American War, War of 1812, World War II, Vietnam, Post World War II, Soldiers

War of 1812, 117–121
West (Region), 122–132, 283–285
Westward Expansion, 122–135
West Virginia, 345–348
Whalers, 255–258
Wiggins, Ella Mae, 217
Wilder, Laura Ingalls, 262, 265, 266
Wisconsin, 349
Women's history, 174, 372–374
World cultures, 375–438
World War II, 172
Work. *See* Occupations
Workers. *See* Occupations
Writing, 7–13

Xiao, 395

Yankee Doodle, 110
Yugoslovia, 384/22

Zaire, 384/17
Zheng, 395
Zimbabwe, 390